PHYGITAL REVOLUTION

THE FUTURE OF MARKETING

APURV ULHAS NAIK

INDIA · SINGAPORE · MALAYSIA

Copyright © Apurv Ulhas Naik 2024
All Rights Reserved.

ISBN
Paperback 979-8-89544-277-7
Hardcase 979-8-89673-313-3

This book has been published with all efforts taken to make the material error-free after the consent of the author. However, the author and the publisher do not assume and hereby disclaim any liability to any party for any loss, damage, or disruption caused by errors or omissions, whether such errors or omissions result from negligence, accident, or any other cause.

While every effort has been made to avoid any mistake or omission, this publication is being sold on the condition and understanding that neither the author nor the publishers or printers would be liable in any manner to any person by reason of any mistake or omission in this publication or for any action taken or omitted to be taken or advice rendered or accepted on the basis of this work. For any defect in printing or binding the publishers will be liable only to replace the defective copy by another copy of this work then available.

Dedication

To my father, whose values and wisdom continue to inspire me every day. To my mother, the energy that inspires me every day to build my dreams. To my elder brother, my lifelong guide and constant source of support. To my wife, my partner, my compass, and my personal philosopher. And to my son, who fills my world with wonder and reminds me that life's best lessons are often the simplest ones.

CONTENTS

INTRODUCTION: WHY DIGITAL AND PHYSICAL MARKETING IS THE FUTURE OF MARKETING

In the dynamic world of marketing, keeping one's senses attuned to the environment is more than just a professional trait; it's a necessity. As a marketer, I constantly observe and analyze the stories other brands tell through their products. Whether I am on the move or merely observing my surroundings, I find myself deeply immersed in the narratives crafted by other marketers. Being an avid consumer myself, I have developed a profound appreciation for the strategic thought and creative effort behind these marketing stories.

One memorable experience that underscored the transformative power of integrating digital and physical marketing occurred during a routine day at Mumbai airport. Fresh from a market visit and eager to return home, I found myself in the bustling atmosphere of the airport. Amidst the rush, I was drawn to an elegantly designed stall just past the duty-free area dedicated to showcasing fragrances.

Curious, I approached the stall where a promoter invited me to "experience" a fragrance. As I sampled the scent, she began to share detailed insights about the fragrance notes and its unique attributes. What truly captured my attention, however, was the next phase of this interaction. The promoter used her mobile device to prompt me to tap a banner on the screen. Within moments, I was answering a few brief questions and providing my feedback.

The efficiency and fluidity of this process were remarkable. While waiting at the baggage counter, my phone buzzed with a message from the fragrance company, expressing gratitude for my participation. Over the following days, I received a series of well-timed WhatsApp messages, each designed to spark my curiosity further. Eventually, this ongoing engagement led me to make several purchases online.

Reflecting on this experience, I came to realize the immense potential of blending physical and digital marketing efforts—a concept I now define as the Phygital Marketing Revolution. This approach not only bridges the gap between two traditionally separate marketing worlds but also creates a seamless continuum that guides consumers from initial discovery to final purchase.

What transpired at that airport stall went beyond a mere sales tactic; it was a testament to how integrating physical and digital elements can forge a compelling and personalized customer journey. While such strategies are currently prevalent in urban settings like airports and metropolitan areas, their potential to extend into rural and remote regions is boundless. Embracing the phygital approach opens new doors for marketers, revolutionizing how we connect with consumers on a broader scale.

PHYGITAL SAMPLING: TRANSFORMING TRADITIONAL OUTREACH

As the marketing head for Society Tea, one of India's most cherished tea brands, I frequently engage in wet sampling to introduce our products to consumers across the country. This outreach is particularly vital in rural areas of Maharashtra and other regions, where direct engagement can significantly impact consumer perceptions. Yet, many companies, including ourselves, often approach sampling with a somewhat traditional mindset. We distribute samples without fully understanding who our consumers are, lacking crucial details such as their names, contact information, or even their preferences. This gap represents a missed opportunity to forge a deeper connection with potential loyal customers.

This is where the concept of Phygital Marketing can revolutionize our approach. By integrating a feedback app into our sampling process, we can gather valuable consumer data in real time. As consumers experience our tea, they can provide immediate feedback through the app, creating an instant digital touchpoint. This integration of physical and digital interactions opens up a realm of possibilities.

The data we collect allows us to create personalized digital experiences for consumers, including tailored messages and discount incentives to drive purchases. The beauty of this approach lies in its ability to sustain the conversation beyond the initial sampling. Consumers who have tasted our product are more likely to respond positively to follow-up messages, especially when these messages reflect their specific preferences.

What was once a straightforward sampling activity transforms into a strategic initiative that drives sales. By converting traditional sampling into a phygital experience, we turn passive tasters into engaged buyers. This blend of digital and physical elements not only enhances the effectiveness of our sampling campaigns but also enables us to build a more data-driven marketing strategy. The result is a more engaged consumer base and a stronger brand presence, even in the most remote parts of India.

A NOTE TO THE READER: BRIDGING THE GAP BETWEEN PHYSICAL AND DIGITAL MARKETING

In today's rapidly evolving marketing landscape, the boundary between physical and digital realms has become increasingly blurred. Successful marketing strategies now thrive on the seamless integration of both domains. This book aims to explore and illuminate the potent synergy that arises when physical and digital marketing efforts are combined, a concept I firmly believe is essential for anyone involved in marketing today.

Throughout these pages, I have endeavored to elucidate the foundational principles of this integration, offering both theoretical and practical insights into how physical and digital worlds can work in harmony to create a cohesive and impactful marketing strategy. My objective is to present this information in a manner that is both accessible and valuable to a broad spectrum of readers.

For students of digital marketing, this book serves as an essential guide, providing a comprehensive overview of how traditional marketing techniques can be enhanced and transformed through digital tools and platforms. My hope is that students will find the content not only informative but also inspiring, encouraging them to think beyond conventional marketing boundaries and explore innovative ways to connect with consumers.

For practicing digital marketers, this book delves into the nuances of integrating physical touchpoints with digital strategies. Whether you are an experienced professional or new to the field, the concepts and case studies presented here are designed to help you refine your approach, stay ahead of industry trends and deliver more effective and memorable marketing campaigns. In a landscape where consumer behavior is continually evolving, the ability to adapt and innovate is crucial. Understanding the interplay between physical and digital marketing is a critical component of that evolution.

Beyond practical application, this book also aims to ignite a broader dialogue about the future of marketing. As we advance, the collaboration between physical and digital elements will become increasingly significant. Marketers will need to adopt a holistic perspective, considering how each touchpoint—whether it be a billboard, a social media ad, a product sample, or a personalized email—contributes to the overall brand experience.

In writing this book, my goal is to provide a valuable resource for anyone looking to deepen their understanding of modern marketing. Whether you are a student eager to learn, a professional seeking to enhance your skills, or simply someone curious about the mechanics of marketing, I believe there is something here for you. The world of marketing is dynamic and ever-changing, but by embracing the synergy between physical and digital elements, we can develop strategies that are not only effective but also enduring and resonant.

1

UNDERSTANDING THE DIGITAL-PHYSICAL DIVIDE

As a marketer navigating the ever-evolving landscape of digital and physical marketing, I find myself constantly reflecting on the remarkable ways these two realms intersect and influence each other. In my career, I've witnessed firsthand how the boundaries between digital and physical marketing have blurred, creating both challenges and opportunities. The rapid advancement of technology has not only transformed how we connect with consumers but also how we need to think about integrating these diverse strategies to create a cohesive and engaging experience.

When I think about the digital-physical divide, I am reminded of the powerful potential that lies in harmonizing these approaches. Digital marketing offers unparalleled precision and adaptability, allowing us to reach audiences with targeted messages in real time. On the other hand, physical marketing provides sensory experiences that foster trust and deepen brand connections in ways that digital alone cannot achieve. The true magic happens when we effectively combine these strengths to craft a seamless journey for the consumer.

Take, for example, Starbucks. The global coffee giant has successfully integrated digital and physical marketing by leveraging its mobile app to enhance the in-store experience. The app allows customers to order ahead, collect rewards, and receive personalized offers, seamlessly bridging the gap between digital engagement and the physical coffeehouse experience. This integration not only boosts convenience for customers but also drives repeat business and brand loyalty.

Similarly, Nike's approach to blending digital and physical experiences is exemplary. The brand's use of digital platforms to drive traffic to its physical stores is a testament to the power of integration. Nike's "NikePlus" membership program offers exclusive content, personalized recommendations, and early access to products, creating a unified experience that extends from online interactions to in-store visits. This cohesive approach helps Nike maintain its position as a leader in both digital and physical spaces.

In the Indian context, brands like Reliance Jio and Nykaa have set benchmarks for integrating digital and physical marketing. Reliance Jio's strategic use of its digital platform to drive foot traffic to its physical stores, along with Nykaa's seamless integration of its online beauty platform with in-store experiences, exemplify how effectively blending these approaches can enhance customer engagement and drive growth.

Reflecting on these examples, it's clear that the divide between digital and physical marketing is not just a challenge, but a significant opportunity. By understanding and embracing the interplay between these two realms, we can craft more holistic and impactful marketing strategies that resonate with today's omnichannel consumers. As we delve deeper into this chapter, I hope to share insights and strategies that will help bridge this divide, drawing from both Indian and international success stories to illustrate the transformative potential of integrated marketing efforts.

INTRODUCTION

In the dynamic and rapidly evolving world of marketing, the once-clear distinctions between digital and physical marketing are increasingly blurred. As consumers seamlessly navigate between online and offline experiences, marketers face both challenges and opportunities in integrating these two realms. This chapter delves into the foundational concepts of digital and physical marketing, explores the changing behaviors of modern consumers, and identifies the challenges and opportunities that arise in bridging the digital-physical divide.

DEFINING DIGITAL AND PHYSICAL MARKETING

Marketing has always been about reaching the right audience at the right time with the right message. Traditionally, this meant leveraging physical channels such as print advertising, billboards, direct mail, and in-store promotions to engage customers. However, with the rapid advancement of technology, digital marketing has emerged as a dominant force, offering new avenues for reaching consumers. Despite the growth of digital marketing, physical marketing remains highly relevant, and the real challenge today is how to integrate these two approaches to create a seamless experience for the consumer.

Digital marketing refers to the use of the internet, mobile devices, social media, search engines and other digital channels to connect with consumers. Key tactics in digital marketing include:

- Content Marketing: Creating valuable and engaging content to attract a target audience. Red Bull India's online magazine, which produces content around extreme sports and adventure, resonates deeply with its target demographic, illustrating how content can drive brand affinity. Similarly, the Indian food brand MTR has utilized content marketing effectively by sharing recipes and cooking tips through its blog and social media channels, enhancing its connection with cooking enthusiasts.

- Social Media Marketing: Utilizing platforms like Facebook, Instagram, and Twitter to engage with consumers. Zomato is a prime example, with its humorous and relatable content that drives high engagement on social media, setting a benchmark in how brands can use personality to build a connection with their audience. Another notable example is Urban Ladder, which engages users through visually appealing content and interactive posts on Instagram, showcasing their furniture designs and home decor ideas.

- Email Marketing: Sending targeted and personalized emails to subscribers. Flipkart uses email campaigns effectively to announce sales, new products, and personalized offers based on customer behavior, thereby driving significant traffic to its platform during key shopping events like Big Billion Day. In a similar vein, Myntra uses personalized emails to update customers about fashion trends and exclusive sales, enhancing customer loyalty and engagement.

- Search Engine Optimization (SEO): Optimizing online content to rank higher in search engine results. MakeMyTrip's investment in SEO to attract travelers searching for holiday packages and travel deals demonstrates how essential visibility in search results is to capturing consumer interest early in the purchase journey. Another example is Ola, which optimizes its website and app content to ensure high-visibility for local taxi services and ride-sharing options.

- Pay-Per-Click (PPC) Advertising: Paying for ad placements on search engines and social media platforms. Amazon India uses PPC advertising extensively to promote specific products, particularly during major shopping events like the Great Indian Festival, ensuring that its offerings are top of mind for consumers ready to buy. Similarly, Reliance Trends leverages PPC ads to highlight its latest fashion collections and in-store promotions.

Physical Marketing, on the other hand, encompasses all offline marketing efforts. These include:

- Print Advertising: Traditional advertisements in newspapers, magazines, brochures, and flyers.

Amul's iconic print ads, which often reflect current events with a humorous twist, have not only become part of Indian popular culture but also demonstrate the enduring power of print to engage audiences. In addition, Hindustan Unilever uses print ads for its product lines, such as Surf Excel, to reach consumers in rural and semi-urban areas.

- Direct Mail: Personalized mail sent directly to potential customers. Big Bazaar's strategy of sending out flyers with offers and discounts to nearby residents has been a successful method of driving foot traffic to its stores, especially during the festive season when consumer spending peaks. Similarly, Shoppers Stop uses direct mail to promote exclusive offers and loyalty programmes to its customers.

- Outdoor Advertising: Billboards, posters, and transit ads seen in public spaces. Tata Motors' use of high-visibility billboards to promote new car models showcases how outdoor advertising remains a powerful tool for building brand awareness, particularly in high-traffic areas. Another example is PepsiCo India, which uses large-scale billboards and bus shelters to advertize its beverages across urban centers.

- Event Marketing: Organizing trade shows, conferences, and live demonstrations to engage directly with consumers. Reliance Jio's launch events, where new technologies and services are demonstrated to large audiences, exemplify how event marketing can create buzz and drive consumer interest in new products. Similarly, the Indian Fashion Week attracts designers, influencers, and fashion enthusiasts, showcasing brands and trends in a high-profile setting.

- In-Store Promotions: Point-of-sale displays, product samples, and special offers within physical retail environments. Godrej Appliances frequently runs in-store promotions, offering demonstrations and discounts that entice customers to experience the products firsthand, thereby driving purchase decisions. Similarly, Pantaloons uses in-store promotions and visual merchandising to enhance the shopping experience and boost sales.

While digital marketing offers precise targeting, measurable results, and the ability to make real-time adjustments, physical marketing provides tangible, sensory experiences that can build trust and strengthen brand recognition. The real key to modern marketing success lies in effectively integrating these two approaches.

CURRENT TRENDS AND CONSUMER BEHAVIORS

In today's marketplace, consumers effortlessly navigate between the digital and physical worlds. They might see an advertisement on Instagram, check out a product review on YouTube, visit a brand's website to compare prices, and finally purchase the product in a physical store. Understanding these fluid behaviors is critical for marketers who aim to create cohesive and effective experiences.

- Omnichannel Behavior: Consumers today expect a seamless experience across all channels. Whether they interact with a brand online or in a physical store, they expect consistency in messaging, pricing, and customer service. Shoppers Stop exemplifies this by integrating its online and offline channels to ensure that customers have a consistent and smooth experience, whether they are browsing online or shopping in-store. Another example is Croma, which provides a seamless omnichannel experience by allowing customers to browse online, check product availability in-store, and enjoy consistent pricing and promotions across platforms.

- Mobile Dominance: The proliferation of smartphones has made consumers always connected, with mobile devices often serving as the bridge between digital and physical experiences. For example, shoppers at Reliance Digital might use their smartphones to look up product information while browsing in-store, blending the digital with the physical seamlessly. Similarly, Tata Sky offers a mobile app that enhances the television viewing experience by allowing users to manage their subscriptions, access content, and receive recommendations.

- Social Proof and Reviews: Online reviews and social media have a significant influence on consumer purchase decisions. Customers often seek validation from other consumers before making a purchase, regardless of whether that purchase is made online or offline. Nykaa, an Indian beauty and wellness retailer, leverages customer reviews and influencer partnerships heavily to build trust and drive sales. Another example is Zivame, which uses customer reviews and testimonials to enhance credibility and encourage purchases.

- Personalization: Today's consumers expect personalized experiences. Brands must understand customer preferences and tailor their communications accordingly, across both digital and physical channels. Tanishq, a leading Indian jewelry brand, offers personalized recommendations based on customer history, both online and in-store, creating a more tailored shopping experience. Similarly, HDFC Bank uses customer data to personalize offers and financial solutions, ensuring relevance and engagement.

- Instant Gratification: The digital age has fostered a culture of instant gratification, where consumers value speed and efficiency. Whether it's fast shipping from an online order or instant information via a mobile app, consumers expect quick results. Swiggy capitalizes on this trend by offering lightning-fast food delivery, meeting the demand for instant gratification. Another example is Paytm, which provides instant payment solutions and quick refunds, catering to the need for immediate financial transactions.

CHALLENGES AND OPPORTUNITIES OF INTEGRATION.

Integrating digital and physical marketing efforts presents a unique set of challenges and opportunities for brands.

Challenges:

1. Data Silos: A common challenge is that data from digital and physical channels are often stored separately, making it difficult to gain a comprehensive view of the customer. For instance, Tata Cliq faces the challenge of integrating data from its online platform with data from its physical stores to create a unified customer profile. Similarly, Big Bazaar must consolidate data from its online promotions and in-store sales to accurately assess customer preferences and behavior.

2. Consistency: Maintaining a consistent brand message and experience across all touchpoints can be particularly challenging, especially when different teams manage digital and physical marketing. FabIndia, with its widespread online presence and numerous physical stores, constantly works to ensure a uniform brand experience for its customers. Another example is Reliance Trends, which strives to maintain consistent branding and customer service across its extensive network of stores and digital platforms.

3. Technology Integration: Ensuring that the various technologies used for digital and physical marketing can communicate and share data seamlessly is another significant challenge. HDFC Bank, for instance, has integrated its online banking services with the experiences provided in its physical branches, ensuring a cohesive customer experience. Similarly, SBI (State Bank of India) integrates its digital banking platform with its physical branch services to offer a unified experience to its customers.

4. Resource Allocation: Effectively balancing investment and resources between digital and physical channels is

critical for optimizing overall marketing performance. DMart, a prominent retail chain in India, carefully allocates resources between its growing online presence and extensive network of physical stores to maintain its competitive pricing and customer satisfaction. Another example is Future Group, which manages its investment between online platforms like Big Bazaar and its brick-and-mortar stores to ensure effective resource utilization.

Opportunities:

1. Enhanced Customer

    Experience: By integrating digital and physical marketing efforts, brands can create a more cohesive and satisfying customer experience, ultimately increasing loyalty and retention. Chumbak, a lifestyle brand, offers a unified shopping experience through its online store and physical outlets, ensuring that customers receive the same quality of service and products across all touchpoints. Another example is PVR Cinemas, which integrates its online ticketing system with in-theater experiences, providing a seamless experience for moviegoers.

2. Better Data Insights: Integration of data across digital and physical channels provides a more comprehensive understanding of customer behaviors and preferences, enabling more effective marketing strategies. Croma, an electronics retail chain, uses integrated data from both online and offline channels to better understand its customers and tailor its marketing efforts accordingly. Similarly, Apollo Hospitals leverages data from its digital health platforms and physical visits to enhance patient care and marketing strategies.

3. Increased Reach: By combining the broad reach of digital marketing with the tangible impact of physical marketing, brands can maximize their exposure and impact. Asian Paints effectively leverages both online and offline channels to reach a wider audience, from television advertisements to digital campaigns and in-store promotions. Another example is Hindustan Aeronautics Limited (HAL), which uses a combination of digital marketing, trade shows, and exhibitions to reach potential clients in the aerospace and defense sectors.

4. Innovative Campaigns: Integration opens up the possibility for more creative and innovative marketing campaigns that leverage the strengths of both digital and physical channels. Cadbury's "Kuch Meetha Ho Jaaye" campaign is a prime example, using a combination of TV ads, online promotions, and in-store displays to create a memorable and impactful marketing effort. Similarly, the "Gully Boy" movie promotion used a blend of digital content, social media buzz, and physical posters to create a comprehensive marketing strategy.

CONCLUSION

By understanding the digital-physical divide, marketers can begin to see how these two realms can complement each other to create a more unified and effective marketing strategy. As we move forward in this book, we will delve into specific strategies and models that can help bridge this divide, allowing marketers to meet the demands of today's omnichannel consumers and create truly integrated marketing campaigns.

2

BUILDING A UNIFIED CUSTOMER EXPERIENCE

In my career as a marketer, one of the most profound realizations has been the importance of delivering a unified customer experience. As consumer expectations evolve, the need for a seamless journey across digital and physical touchpoints has never been more critical. This realization has profoundly influenced my approach to marketing, highlighting the significance of creating a cohesive experience that resonates with customers at every interaction.

Building a unified customer experience is not just about aligning marketing messages across channels; it's about weaving together digital and physical elements into a harmonious whole that meets and exceeds customer expectations. The challenge lies in ensuring that every touchpoint, whether online or offline, contributes to a consistent and engaging brand experience.

Reflecting on this, I'm inspired by several international brands that have excelled in creating seamless customer experiences. For example, Apple has mastered the art of integrating its digital and physical touchpoints. The Apple Store experience is meticulously designed to reflect the brand's digital ethos, with online orders seamlessly transitioning into in-store pickups and support. This integration ensures that customers encounter a consistent brand experience, whether interacting through the website, mobile app, or physical store.

Similarly, Starbucks has excelled in creating a unified customer journey through its mobile app and physical stores. The Starbucks app not only allows customers to order and pay ahead but also integrates with the loyalty program, offering personalized rewards and promotions based on purchase history. This seamless experience enhances customer satisfaction and fosters brand loyalty.

Another exemplary case is Nike, which has successfully integrated its digital and physical channels through the Nike+ ecosystem. The Nike app connects with physical stores to provide a personalized shopping experience, including exclusive product launches and in-store events tailored to the customer's interests. This integration enhances the customer's journey, blending digital convenience with physical engagement.

In my role as a marketer, these examples underscore the importance of creating a unified experience that aligns with modern consumer expectations. The key lies in understanding the interplay between digital and physical touchpoints, and leveraging this knowledge to craft a seamless and engaging journey for customers.

As we delve into the principles of building a unified customer experience in this chapter, I hope to provide valuable insights and practical strategies that will help bridge the gap between digital and physical interactions, ultimately creating a more cohesive and compelling brand experience.

INTRODUCTION

In today's fast-paced and interconnected world, delivering a seamless customer journey is paramount for businesses aiming to thrive in the competitive marketplace. Whether a customer interacts with a brand online or offline, their experience should be consistent, cohesive and enjoyable. A unified customer experience not only enhances customer satisfaction but also builds loyalty, fosters brand advocacy and drives long-term business success. This chapter delves into the principles of creating a seamless customer journey, with a special focus on examples from Indian businesses that have successfully integrated their digital and physical marketing efforts.

Principles of Creating a Seamless Customer Journey

1. Customer-Centric Approach.

   A customer-centric approach is the cornerstone of a successful marketing strategy. It involves putting the customer at the center of all marketing efforts and making decisions based on a deep understanding of their needs, preferences, and behaviors. For instance, Titan Company, a leading Indian watch and jewelry retailer, has built its brand around a customer-first philosophy. By leveraging customer feedback and data, Titan continually refines its product offerings and customer service to align with evolving consumer expectations.

- Understanding Customer Needs: Use customer feedback, surveys, and data analytics to gain insights into what customers value most.

- Personalization: Tailor marketing messages and experiences to individual customer preferences, whether they are browsing your website or visiting a physical store.

- Continuous Improvement: Regularly update your strategies based on customer feedback, to ensure that the customer journey remains relevant and engaging.

2. Consistency Across Channels

Consistency across all channels is crucial for building trust and brand recognition. Customers expect the same level of service, product information, and pricing whether they are engaging with a brand online or offline. Tata CLiQ, Tata Group's e-commerce platform, ensures that its branding, messaging, and customer service are consistent across its website, mobile app, and physical stores, creating a seamless experience for its customers.

- Brand Message: Maintain a consistent tone of voice, visual identity, and brand values across all marketing channels.

- Uniform Pricing and Offers: Ensure that promotional offers, product information, and pricing are aligned across digital and physical platforms.

- Cross-Channel Communication: Keep customers informed and engaged by delivering consistent messages through email, social media, in-store signage, and other channels.

3. Integration of Digital and Physical Touchpoints

Identifying and integrating key touchpoints where customers interact with your brand is essential for creating a seamless experience. Shoppers Stop, one of India's leading retail chains, exemplifies this by offering an integrated shopping experience where customers can browse products online, check availability in nearby stores, and choose between home delivery or in-store pickup.

- Mapping the Customer Journey: Identify all the touchpoints where customers interact with your brand, from social media and websites to physical stores, and customer service.

- Connecting Touchpoints: Find ways to connect these touchpoints seamlessly, such as offering online purchase and in-store pickup options, or integrating customer data across platforms.

- Omnichannel Strategy: Develop an omnichannel strategy that allows customers to transition smoothly between online and offline experiences.

4. Personalization and Relevance

Personalization is key to creating a meaningful and relevant customer experience. By leveraging customer data from both digital and physical interactions, brands can offer personalized recommendations, targeted ads, and tailored in-store experiences. Myntra, a popular fashion e-commerce platform in India, uses advanced algorithms to analyse customer behavior and preferences, enabling it to deliver personalized product recommendations and marketing messages.

- **Data-Driven Personalization:** Use customer data to deliver personalized experiences, such as recommending products based on previous purchases, or tailoring email campaigns to individual interests.

- **Holistic Customer View:** Integrate customer data from all touchpoints to create a comprehensive view of each customer, enabling more effective personalization.

- **Relevance in Communication:** Ensure that all communications, whether online or in-store, are relevant to the customer's needs and preferences.

5. Omnichannel Accessibility

In today's interconnected world, customers expect to interact with brands through multiple channels and switch between them effortlessly. Reliance Retail, India's largest retailer, has successfully implemented an omnichannel strategy by allowing customers to shop online, reserve products, and pick them up at a nearby store, providing a seamless experience across digital and physical channels.

- Multiple Access Points: Ensure that customers can access your brand through various channels, including websites, mobile apps, social media, and physical stores.

- Seamless Transitions: Enable customers to switch between channels without disruption, such as starting a purchase online and completing it in-store.

- Consistent Support: Provide consistent customer support across all channels, whether through chatbots, call centers, or in-store assistance.

KEY TOUCHPOINTS AND THEIR INTEGRATION.

To build a unified customer experience, it's essential to identify and integrate key touchpoints in the customer journey. These touchpoints can be broadly categorized into digital and physical interactions:

1. Digital Touchpoints:

   - Website and Mobile App: Your online presence is often the first point of contact for customers. Ensure that your website and app are user-friendly, informative, and consistent with your brand's identity. Zivame, India's leading lingerie brand, offers an intuitive website and mobile app that provide a seamless browsing and shopping experience, with features like virtual try-ons and personalized size recommendations.

   - Social Media: Platforms like Facebook, Instagram, Twitter, and LinkedIn are critical for engaging with customers, sharing content, and building community. Durex India effectively uses social media to engage with its audience through witty content, promotions, and user-generated content campaigns.

- Email Marketing: Personalized and relevant email campaigns can drive engagement and sales. Flipkart uses email marketing to announce sales, new products, and personalized offers based on previous customer behavior, ensuring a targeted and effective communication strategy.

- Online Advertising: Paid ads on search engines and social media can attract new customers and drive traffic to your website or physical stores. Ola, India's popular ride-hailing app, uses targeted online ads to reach potential customers and encourage app downloads.

- Customer Service Chatbots: Providing instant support through chatbots on your website or app can enhance customer satisfaction and resolve issues quickly. HDFC Bank uses AI-powered chatbots to assist customers with banking queries, providing instant support, and improving the overall customer experience.

2. Physical Touchpoints:

- Brick-and-Mortar Stores: In-store experiences should reflect the same branding and customer service quality as your digital channels. Fabindia, known for its ethnic wear and home products, creates an inviting in-store environment that complements its online presence, offering personalized service and an immersive shopping experience.

- Events and Trade Shows: Hosting or participating in events allows for direct interaction with customers, offering hands-on experiences with your products and brand. Godrej frequently participates in trade shows and exhibitions where customers can experience their home appliances and furniture first hand.

- Printed Materials: Brochures, catalogs, and direct mail can complement digital efforts, driving customers to your online platforms or physical locations. Big Bazaar often sends out flyers with discounts and offers to nearby residents, driving foot traffic to their stores.

- Customer Service Centers: Providing excellent service through call centers or in-store support can significantly impact customer loyalty. Airtel, one of India's leading telecom companies, offers robust customer support through its call centers and In-store service centers, ensuring a positive experience across all touchpoints.

INTEGRATION STRATEGIES:

To effectively integrate digital and physical touchpoints, brands need to employ strategies that ensure a seamless customer journey:

1.   Unified Data Systems:

- Integrated CRM Systems: Use integrated CRM (Customer Relationship Management) systems to collect and analyze data from all touchpoints. Croma, India's leading electronics retailer, uses integrated data systems to gain a comprehensive understanding of customer behavior and preferences, enabling personalized marketing efforts.

- Customer Data Integration: Consolidate data from online and offline channels to create a unified customer profile, enabling more effective targeting and personalization.

2.   Cross-Channel Promotions:

- Synchronized Offers: Ensure that promotional offers are synchronized across digital and physical channels. Domino's Pizza India offers online discounts that are also available in-store, creating a consistent experience for customers.

- Omnichannel Campaigns: Develop marketing campaigns that span multiple channels, reinforcing the brand message and ensuring that customers encounter consistent offers and messaging.

3.   Seamless Transitions:

- Online Purchase, In-Store Pickup: Offer options for online purchase and in-store pickup, as seen with Decathlon India, where customers can order sports equipment online and collect it at a nearby store.

- QR Codes and Digital Integration: Provide QR codes in-store that link to online product details, as done by Tanishq, where customers can scan QR codes to view jewelry details and reviews online.

4. Consistent Messaging:

- Aligned Communication: Ensure that all marketing messages, whether digital or physical, are aligned and reinforce each other. Cadbury India successfully aligns its TV ads, social media campaigns, and in-store displays to create a cohesive marketing message.

Techniques for Maintaining Consistency Across Channels.

Consistency is the key to a unified customer experience. Here are some techniques to ensure consistency across digital and physical channels:

1. Brand Guidelines:

- Comprehensive Guidelines: Develop and maintain comprehensive brand guidelines that cover visual identity, tone of voice, and messaging. Maruti Suzuki maintains strict brand guidelines to ensure consistent communication across all its dealerships and marketing channels.

- Regular Updates: Regularly update the guidelines to reflect any changes in branding or marketing strategy, ensuring all teams are aligned.

2. Centralized Content Management:

- Content Consistency: Use a centralized content management system (CMS) to ensure that all marketing content is consistent and up-to-date across all channels. ICICI Bank employs a robust CMS to manage its online and offline content, ensuring that the information customers receive is uniform across its website, mobile app, and printed materials.

- Coordination and Distribution: Coordinate content creation and distribution across various teams to maintain a cohesive message. This is particularly important in large organizations with multiple departments and regional offices.

3. Integrated Marketing Campaigns:

- Multi-Channel Campaigns: Plan and execute marketing campaigns that span multiple channels, ensuring that each channel supports and reinforces the others. Amul excels in this area, with its advertising campaigns often appearing across television, print, digital, and outdoor media, all carrying the same iconic messaging.

- Physical-Digital Synergy: Use a mix of digital and physical marketing tactics to reach customers wherever they are. Patanjali Ayurved effectively blends physical and digital marketing by combining TV ads with a strong social media presence and on-ground promotions.

4. Employee Training and Communication:

- Brand Training: Train employees across all departments on brand standards and the importance of consistency in customer interactions. Starbucks India ensures that its staff are well-versed in brand guidelines and customer service standards, which helps deliver a consistent experience in every outlet.

- **Inter-Departmental Communication:** Foster open communication between teams responsible for digital and physical marketing to ensure alignment. Raymond has successfully implemented this by integrating its digital and retail teams, ensuring that promotions and customer experiences are synchronized across online and offline platforms.

5. **Customer Feedback Loops:**

- **Continuous Feedback Collection:** Collect feedback from customers about their experiences with your brand across different channels. Bigbasket frequently gathers customer feedback on its website and mobile app to understand user experience and improve its service accordingly.

- **Feedback-Driven Improvements:** Use this feedback to identify inconsistencies and areas for improvement. Implement systems for continuously gathering and analyzing customer feedback, ensuring that your brand remains responsive to customer needs.

6. **Performance Monitoring and Adjustment:**

- **Analytics and Metrics:** Regularly monitor the performance of your marketing efforts across all channels. Use analytics tools to track key metrics, such as customer satisfaction, engagement rates, and conversion rates. Jio (Reliance Jio) utilizes advanced analytics to monitor the performance of its marketing campaigns across digital and physical channels, adjusting strategies based on real-time data.

- Agility in Strategy: Be prepared to adjust strategies and tactics based on performance data to maintain consistency and effectiveness. Nykaa, an Indian beauty retailer, frequently tweaks its digital campaigns based on performance metrics to ensure that its messaging resonates with its target audience.

CASE STUDIES: INDIAN BUSINESSES LEADING THE WAY

To further illustrate the application of these principles, let's look at a few Indian businesses that have successfully integrated their digital and physical marketing efforts to create a unified customer experience:

1. Tata Motors:

    - Seamless Brand Experience: Tata Motors has effectively integrated its online and offline channels by offering virtual showrooms where customers can explore vehicles online before visiting a physical dealership. The brand ensures that the information provided online, such as pricing, features, and promotions, is consistent with what customers experience in-store. This integration allows Tata Motors to offer a seamless and consistent brand experience across all touchpoints.

2. FabAlley:

    *   Omnichannel Strategy: FabAlley, an Indian fashion brand, has embraced an omnichannel strategy by integrating its online platform with physical stores. Customers can browse the latest collections online, place orders for home delivery, or pick up their purchases at a nearby store. Additionally, FabAlley uses customer data from both online and offline interactions to provide personalized recommendations, creating a cohesive shopping experience that bridges the digital-physical divide.

3. Asian Paints:

    *   Holistic Customer Journey: Asian Paints has developed a customer journey that seamlessly integrates digital and physical touchpoints. Through its website and mobile app, customers can explore a wide range of products, visualize color combinations in their homes, and even schedule a visit from a color consultant. In physical stores, the brand offers a similar experience with interactive displays and expert advice, ensuring that the customer journey remains consistent and personalized across all channels.

4. Reliance Retail's Ajio:

    *   Cross-Channel Engagement: Ajio, the fashion and lifestyle brand from Reliance Retail, has

successfully integrated its online presence with offline experiences. Customers can browse collections online, take advantage of special offers, and choose to have their purchases delivered to their homes or pick them up at a nearby Reliance store. Ajio also engages customers through social media, email campaigns and in-store events, creating a unified and engaging customer experience.

5. Haldiram's:

- Consistent Brand Messaging: Haldiram's, a popular Indian sweets and snacks brand, has maintained consistency across its digital and physical channels. Whether customers are visiting a Haldiram's store, ordering online, or interacting with the brand on social media, they experience the same messaging, quality, and service. Haldiram's has also successfully integrated its e-commerce platform with physical outlets, allowing customers to enjoy a unified shopping experience.

CONCLUSION

Building a unified customer experience requires a strategic approach that seamlessly integrates digital and physical marketing efforts. By focusing on the principles outlined in this chapter—such as maintaining consistency across channels, personalizing customer interactions, and integrating key touchpoints—Indian businesses can create a cohesive and enjoyable customer journey that drives brand loyalty and long-term success. The examples of Indian businesses provided here demonstrate that it is possible to bridge the digital-physical divide effectively, resulting in a more engaged and satisfied customer base. As the marketplace continues to evolve, brands that prioritize a unified customer experience will be well-positioned to thrive in the competitive landscape.

3

THE DIGITAL-PHYSICAL INTEGRATION MODEL

As a marketer navigating the evolving landscape of branding and consumer engagement, the quest to develop an effective Digital-Physical Integration Model has become a central focus of my strategic efforts. The rapid convergence of digital and physical marketing realms presents both a significant challenge and a remarkable opportunity. It has become increasingly clear that integrating these two domains is essential for creating cohesive and impactful customer experiences.

In my journey, I've come to appreciate the intricacies involved in melding digital and physical marketing strategies. The integration model is not just a theoretical concept, but a practical framework that can drive real-world success. This model emphasizes the need for a seamless blend of online and offline interactions, ensuring that every consumer touchpoint contributes to a unified brand experience.

One of the key lessons I've learned is that successful integration requires a strategic approach that leverages the strengths of both digital and physical channels. For instance, consider how Starbucks has masterfully integrated its digital and physical presence. Through its mobile app, Starbucks not only allows customers to order and pay in advance, but also provides a personalized experience with rewards and offers that drive both digital engagement and in-store visits. This integration creates a seamless journey from the online ordering process to the physical pickup, enhancing customer convenience and satisfaction.

Another powerful example is Nike's use of its Nike+ ecosystem. Nike integrates its digital platforms, including the Nike Run Club app, with its physical stores and products. The app tracks users' workouts and provides personalized recommendations, while physical stores offer exclusive in-store experiences and events that complement the digital engagement. This integration fosters a deeper connection with customers by blending their digital and physical interactions into a cohesive brand experience.

Brands like Apple also provide valuable insights into effective integration. Apple's approach to integrating its digital and physical channels is exemplified by the seamless experience offered through its Apple Store app. Customers can explore products online, schedule appointments for in-store consultations, and receive personalized support, creating a fluid transition between the digital and physical realms. This model not only enhances the customer experience but also reinforces brand loyalty.

In my role, I have witnessed the transformative impact of applying a well-crafted integration model. By aligning digital and physical strategies, brands can create a more engaging and consistent customer journey, driving higher levels of satisfaction and loyalty. This chapter aims to explore the principles and practices of the Digital-Physical Integration Model, offering insights and strategies that can be applied to enhance marketing efforts and build stronger connections with consumers.

As we delve into the framework of this model, I encourage you to reflect on how these principles can be adapted to your own marketing strategies. Embracing an integrated approach allows us to bridge the gap between digital and physical experiences, ultimately delivering a more cohesive and impactful brand interaction. By leveraging examples from leading international brands, we can gain valuable insights into creating a successful integration model that meets the needs of today's omnichannel consumers.

INTRODUCING THE MODEL: COMPONENTS AND FRAMEWORK

Integrating digital and physical marketing efforts requires a comprehensive and structured approach. The Digital-Physical Integration Model offers a robust framework to guide marketers in creating a seamless strategy that harmonizes online and offline touchpoints. This model encompasses several crucial components:

1. Customer-Centric Foundation

    - Understanding Your Audience: To effectively blend digital and physical marketing, start with an in-depth understanding of your audience. Conduct thorough research using tools such as surveys, focus groups, and advanced data analytics to gather insights into customer needs, preferences, and behaviors. For instance, Tata Tea employs sophisticated data analytics to tailor its marketing strategies, ensuring they resonate with diverse consumer segments.

- Segmentation and Personas: Develop detailed customer personas that represent various segments of your audience. These personas should encompass demographic data, behavioral traits, and channel preferences. For example, HDFC Bank creates personas based on customer data to tailor their marketing messages across different platforms, enhancing engagement and relevance.

2. Unified Brand Identity

- Consistent Branding: Ensure that your brand's visual identity, messaging, and tone of voice are consistent across all channels. This includes logos, colors, fonts, and key messages. A notable example is the Indian e-commerce giant, Flipkart, which maintains a consistent brand identity across its digital platforms and physical retail experiences, reinforcing brand recognition and trust.

- Brand Storytelling: Craft a compelling brand story that resonates with your audience and can be communicated seamlessly across digital and physical platforms. For instance, Amul's storytelling through its iconic advertisements and packaging helps create a memorable brand image that spans both offline and online touchpoints.

3. Integrated Marketing Strategy

- Channel Selection: Identify the most effective digital and physical channels for reaching your target audience. Consider factors such as audience preferences, channel capabilities, and cost-effectiveness. For example, Maruti Suzuki uses a mix of digital advertising and physical dealership promotions to effectively reach and engage potential car buyers.

- Content Coordination: Develop a content strategy that aligns with your brand identity and is adaptable across different channels. Ensure that content created for digital platforms can be repurposed for physical marketing, and vice versa. A case in point is how Nykaa integrates its online beauty content with in-store experiences to enhance customer engagement.

- Campaign Synchronization: Plan marketing campaigns that leverage both digital and physical touchpoints. Coordinate timing, messaging and offers to create a cohesive experience for customers. The Big Bazaar "Sabse Saste Din" sale effectively integrates online promotions with in-store events to drive footfall and online traffic.

4. Data Integration and Analytics

- Unified Data Systems: Implement integrated CRM (Customer Relationship Management) and marketing automation systems that consolidate data from all touchpoints. This provides a single view of the customer and enables more effective targeting and personalization. Companies like Reliance Jio use integrated data systems to enhance customer experience and drive personalized marketing strategies.

- Data-Driven Insights: Use data analytics to monitor customer interactions, track campaign performance, and identify trends. Leverage these insights to refine your marketing strategies and enhance the customer experience. For instance, Amazon India utilizes advanced analytics to track customer behavior and tailor its marketing efforts for improved results.

5. Technology and Tools

- Marketing Automation: Utilize marketing automation platforms to streamline campaign management, personalization, and data collection. These tools can help coordinate efforts across digital and physical channels. Companies like Zomato leverage marketing automation to manage their extensive digital campaigns and integrate them with offline promotions effectively.

- Customer Experience Management (CXM): Implement CXM solutions to manage and optimize customer interactions across all touchpoints. These tools can provide real-time insights and support personalized engagement. For example, Tata Motors uses CXM solutions to enhance customer interactions at various touchpoints, from online inquiries to dealership visits.

- Point-of-Sale (POS) Systems: Integrate POS systems with digital platforms to ensure a seamless transition between online and offline transactions. This enables features like online order pickup, in-store inventory checks, and unified customer profiles. Companies like Big Bazaar and Lifestyle leverage integrated POS systems to enhance the shopping experience, both online and in-store.

6. Cross-Channel Customer Engagement

- Omnichannel Communication: Develop a communication strategy that ensures customers receive consistent and relevant messages across all channels. Use email, social media, SMS, and in-store signage to deliver a unified experience. For example, Puma India maintains a cohesive communication strategy across social media, email marketing and physical stores to engage with its audience effectively.

- Personalization: Personalize interactions based on customer data and preferences. Tailor offers, content, and recommendations to individual customers to enhance engagement and satisfaction. Companies like BigBasket use customer data to personalize promotions and recommendations, both online and in-store.

7. Measurement and Optimization

- Key Performance Indicators (KPIs): Define KPIs for both digital and physical marketing efforts. Common metrics include customer acquisition cost, lifetime value, conversion rates, and customer satisfaction. For example, MakeMyTrip tracks KPIs such as booking conversion rates and customer satisfaction scores to gauge the effectiveness of its integrated marketing strategies.

- Continuous Improvement: Regularly review performance data to identify areas for improvement. Conduct A/B testing, gather customer feedback, and iterate on strategies to optimize results. For instance, Swiggy continually refines its marketing strategies based on performance data and customer feedback to enhance its market position.

STEPS TO IMPLEMENT THE MODEL IN YOUR ORGANIZATION

Implementing the Digital-Physical Integration Model involves several strategic steps. Here's a guide to help you get started:

1. Assessment and Planning

- Current State Analysis: Evaluate your existing marketing efforts, identifying strengths, weaknesses, and gaps in integration. Assess the effectiveness of your digital and physical channels. For example, Hindustan Unilever assesses its marketing mix to identify areas for better integration between digital campaigns and in-store promotions.

- Goal Setting: Define clear objectives for your integration efforts. Consider goals such as improving customer experience, increasing engagement, and driving sales growth. Set measurable goals, like enhancing brand recall, or boosting online-to-offline conversion rates.

- Resource Allocation: Determine the resources needed to implement the model, including budget, technology, and personnel. Allocate resources strategically to support integration efforts. For instance, companies like Unacademy invest in both technology and talent to enhance their digital and physical marketing integration.

2. Customer Insights and Segmentation

- Data Collection: Gather data from both digital and physical channels to build a comprehensive understanding of your customers. Use surveys, analytics, and CRM data to inform your insights. For example, LG Electronics collects data from various touchpoints to tailor its marketing strategies and improve customer satisfaction.

- Segmentation: Segment your audience based on key characteristics and behaviors. Develop detailed personas to guide your marketing efforts. Companies like P&G use segmentation to target different customer groups with tailored messaging and offers.

3. Developing a Unified Strategy

- Channel Integration: Identify opportunities for integrating digital and physical channels. For example, offer in-store promotions that are advertized online, or use QR codes in physical stores to drive online engagement. Reliance Digital uses QR codes and online coupons to bridge the gap between its online platform and physical stores.

- Content Planning: Create a content calendar that aligns with your integrated strategy. Plan campaigns that leverage both digital and physical touchpoints, ensuring consistent messaging and timing. Companies like Myntra plan their marketing content to align with major sales events, integrating both online ads and physical store promotions.

- Technology Integration: Implement the necessary technologies to support integration. This may include CRM systems, marketing automation platforms, and CXM solutions. For instance, Ola integrates its digital app with physical touchpoints, like ride-hailing kiosks, to enhance customer convenience.

4.   Execution and Coordination

- **Cross-Functional Collaboration:** Foster collaboration between teams responsible for digital and physical marketing. Ensure regular communication and coordination to align efforts. Companies like Berger Paints encourage cross-functional teams to work together on integrated campaigns, enhancing overall effectiveness.

- **Campaign Management:** Execute integrated campaigns according to your plan. Monitor performance in real time and make adjustments as needed to optimize results. For example, PepsiCo monitors its integrated campaigns across TV, digital, and in-store channels to ensure alignment and effectiveness.

5.   Measurement and Optimization

- **Performance Tracking:** Use analytics tools to track the performance of your integrated marketing efforts. Monitor KPIs and gather insights to inform future strategies. For instance, Godrej tracks KPIs, such as brand engagement and sales conversion rates, to evaluate the success of its integrated marketing strategies.

- **Continuous Improvement:** Regularly review and refine your integration efforts based on performance data and customer feedback. Conduct A/B testing and iterate on strategies to achieve better results. Companies like Cadbury refine their marketing approaches based on consumer feedback and performance metrics.

TOOLS AND TECHNOLOGIES FOR INTEGRATION

Effective integration of digital and physical marketing efforts relies on the right tools and technologies. Here are some key solutions to consider:

1. Customer Relationship Management (CRM) systems

   - CRM systems help consolidate customer data from all touchpoints, providing a single view of the customer. This enables personalized marketing and better customer insights. For example, SBI uses CRM systems to manage customer interactions and personalize its marketing efforts.

2. Marketing Automation Platforms

   - Marketing automation platforms streamline campaign management, allowing you to coordinate efforts across digital and physical channels. These tools support email marketing, social media, lead nurturing and more. Companies like Netmeds use marketing automation to integrate their digital campaigns with physical store promotions.

3. Customer Experience Management (CXM) Solutions

   - CXM solutions help manage and optimize customer interactions across all touchpoints. These tools provide real-time insights and support personalized engagement, enhancing the overall customer experience. For instance, Royal Enfield uses CXM solutions to enhance its customer interactions across its showrooms and online platforms.

4. Point-of-Sale (POS) Systems

- Integrating POS systems with digital platforms enables seamless transitions between online and offline transactions. Features like online order pickup, in-store inventory checks, and unified customer profiles are made possible with integrated POS systems. Brands like Lifestyle and Shoppers Stop utilize integrated POS systems to provide a smooth shopping experience.

5. Analytics and Data Visualization Tools.

- Analytics tools help track performance across channels, providing insights into customer behavior, campaign effectiveness, and overall marketing ROI. Data visualization tools make it easier to interpret and act on these insights. Companies like Bajaj Finserv use analytics tools to monitor campaign performance and customer interactions.

6. Content Management Systems (CMS).

- A CMS helps manage and distribute content consistently across all channels. It ensures that your brand messaging remains cohesive and up-to-date. Companies like HDFC Life use CMS platforms to maintain consistent messaging across their website, social media and physical marketing materials.

- By leveraging these tools and technologies, you can effectively integrate digital and physical marketing efforts, creating a unified and engaging customer experience.

4

STRATEGY DEVELOPMENT AND EXECUTION

In the ever-evolving world of marketing, the art of strategy development and execution is where vision meets reality. As a marketer dedicated to bridging the digital-physical divide, I have come to realize that crafting and executing a cohesive strategy is not just about setting goals, but about orchestrating a symphony of aligned efforts that drive impactful results. This chapter delves into the essence of strategy development and execution, drawing from my experiences and observations in the dynamic field of marketing.

Reflecting on my journey, I've learned that effective strategy development requires a deep understanding of both the digital and physical landscapes. It's about aligning goals, optimizing resources, and executing plans that resonate across various touchpoints. For instance, witnessing Nike's seamless integration of its digital and physical marketing efforts has been particularly enlightening. Nike's ability to align its online presence with in-store experiences, such as through its personalized NikePlus membership program and innovative in-store technologies, showcases the power of a unified strategy in driving customer engagement and loyalty.

Another compelling example is Starbucks, which has mastered the art of aligning its digital strategy with its physical stores. The Starbucks Rewards program, which integrates mobile ordering, personalized offers, and in-store experiences, demonstrates how a well-executed strategy can enhance customer convenience and satisfaction. Starbucks' ability to execute this strategy across its global network of stores highlights the importance of consistency and coherence in delivering a superior customer experience.

In the luxury sector, Louis Vuitton's approach to strategy development and execution offers valuable insights. By aligning its digital marketing campaigns with exclusive in-store events and personalized customer experiences, Louis Vuitton creates a seamless and cohesive brand experience that resonates with its high-end clientele. The integration of digital storytelling with physical store presentations exemplifies how luxury brands can successfully merge online and offline efforts to reinforce their brand identity and drive customer engagement.

My experiences have reinforced the belief that strategy development and execution are about more than just creating plans; they're about bringing those plans to life through meticulous execution and alignment. It involves setting clear objectives, leveraging data-driven insights, and continuously refining approaches to meet evolving consumer expectations.

As we explore the principles and practices of strategy development and execution in this chapter, I invite you to reflect on how these concepts can be applied to your own marketing efforts. The goal is to create a cohesive strategy that effectively integrates digital and physical touchpoints, ensuring that every aspect of your marketing efforts works together to drive meaningful results.

In essence, this chapter represents a journey into the heart of strategic marketing – a journey that I have found both challenging and rewarding. By delving into international case studies and real-world examples, I hope to provide valuable insights and practical guidance that will help you navigate the complexities of strategy development and execution, ultimately leading to more impactful and cohesive marketing campaigns.

CRAFTING A COHESIVE MARKETING STRATEGY

Developing a cohesive marketing strategy that integrates both digital and physical efforts requires meticulous planning and execution. The following steps provide a comprehensive approach to create a unified strategy:

1. Define Clear Objectives

   - Set Measurable Goals: Establish specific, measurable, achievable, relevant, and time-bound (SMART) goals for your marketing efforts. These can include increasing brand awareness, driving sales, enhancing customer engagement, or improving customer retention. For instance,

Tata Motors sets clear SMART goals for its marketing campaigns to boost brand visibility and sales.

- Align with Business Objectives: Ensure that your marketing goals are in alignment with overall business objectives. This alignment helps in securing organizational support and necessary resources. For example, Hindustan Unilever aligns its marketing strategies with its business goals of sustainability and growth.

2. Understand Your Audience

- Market Research: Conduct thorough market research to gather insights about your target audience. Use surveys, focus groups, and social listening tools to understand their needs, preferences, and behaviors. Companies like Mahindra & Mahindra invest in comprehensive market research to better understand customer demands and market trends.

- Customer Segmentation: Segment your audience based on demographics, psychographics, and behavioral data. Develop detailed personas to represent each segment and guide your marketing efforts. For example, Flipkart segments its audience based on shopping behavior and preferences to tailor its marketing campaigns effectively.

3. Develop Key Messages

- Brand Messaging: Create key messages that effectively communicate your brand's value proposition, mission, and vision. Ensure that these messages resonate with your target audience and differentiate your brand from competitors. For instance, Bajaj Finserv emphasizes its customer-centric messaging to highlight its financial services and solutions.

- Consistency: Maintain consistency in messaging across all channels. This consistency reinforces your brand identity and builds trust with your audience. Companies like Britannia ensure their messaging is consistent across TV ads, social media, and packaging, to strengthen brand recognition.

4. Select the Right Channels

- Channel Analysis: Evaluate the effectiveness of various digital and physical channels for reaching your target audience. Consider factors such as audience preferences, channel capabilities, and cost-effectiveness. For example, Jio has effectively used a mix of digital ads and physical retail presence to reach a broad audience.

- Integrated Channel Strategy: Develop an integrated channel strategy that leverages the strengths of both digital and physical channels. For example, use digital channels for awareness and engagement, and physical channels for experiential marketing and direct sales. Brands like Big Bazaar combine online promotions with in-store events to drive sales.

5. Content Planning and Creation

- **Content Strategy:** Develop a content strategy that aligns with your brand messaging and supports your marketing goals. Plan content that can be adapted for both digital and physical channels. For instance, Zomato creates engaging content for its app and integrates it with physical marketing in restaurants.

- **Content Calendar:** Create a content calendar to schedule and coordinate content across channels. Ensure that content is timely, relevant, and engaging for your audience. Companies like Nykaa use content calendars to synchronize their online campaigns with offline events.

6. Budget Allocation

- **Resource Planning:** Allocate budget and resources strategically across digital and physical channels. Consider the potential return on investment (ROI) for each channel and prioritize accordingly. For example, Unacademy allocates its budget based on the performance of digital campaigns and offline promotional events.

- **Flexibility:** Maintain flexibility in your budget to adapt to changing market conditions and emerging opportunities. Brands like Maruti Suzuki adjust their budgets dynamically based on market trends and promotional needs.

ALIGNING DIGITAL AND PHYSICAL MARKETING GOALS

To ensure that digital and physical marketing efforts work toward common objectives, it is crucial to align their goals. Here's how to achieve this alignment:

1. Unified Planning Process

    - Collaborative Planning: Involve both digital and physical marketing teams in the planning process. Encourage collaboration and open communication to ensure that all efforts are aligned. For example, brands like Parle-G ensure cross-functional collaboration between their digital and offline teams to synchronize campaigns.

    - Integrated Campaigns: Design integrated marketing campaigns that leverage both digital and physical touchpoints. Coordinate timing, messaging, and offers to create a seamless customer experience. Companies like Airtel run integrated campaigns that combine TV ads, digital promotions, and in-store offers.

2. Common Metrics and KPIs

    - Define Metrics: Establish common metrics and key performance indicators (KPIs) to measure the success of both digital and physical marketing efforts. Examples include customer acquisition cost, conversion rates, customer lifetime value, and customer satisfaction. For instance, ICICI Bank tracks KPIs across its online and offline channels to evaluate campaign effectiveness.

- Performance Tracking: Use analytics tools to track performance across channels. Regularly review and analyze data to identify trends and areas for improvement. Companies like HDFC Life use analytics to assess the performance of their integrated marketing strategies.

3. Customer Journey Mapping

- Identify Touchpoints: Map out the customer journey to identify key touchpoints where customers interact with your brand. This includes both digital and physical interactions. For example, Tata Tea maps customer interactions from online engagement to in-store purchases to enhance the customer journey.

- Seamless Transitions: Ensure that customers can move seamlessly between digital and physical touchpoints. For example, enable online purchase and in-store pickup, or provide QR codes in-store that link to online content. Brands like Lifestyle use QR codes and mobile apps to create a seamless shopping experience.

4. Consistent Customer Experience

- Training and Support: Train employees across all departments to deliver a consistent customer experience. This includes customer service, sales, and marketing teams. For example, Café Coffee Day trains its staff to ensure a uniform customer experience across all its locations.

- Customer Feedback: Collect and analyse customer feedback to identify areas where the customer experience can be improved. Use this feedback to inform future strategies and initiatives. Companies like Spencers Retail use customer feedback to refine their service offerings and improve the overall shopping experience.

CASE STUDIES OF SUCCESSFUL STRATEGY IMPLEMENTATIONS

Examining real-world examples of successful digital-physical integration can provide valuable insights and inspiration. Here are a few detailed case studies:

CASE STUDY 1: NIKE

- Objective: Nike aimed to create a seamless customer experience that integrates online and offline interactions.

- Strategy: Nike implemented several initiatives to achieve this goal, including:

- NikePlus Membership: A loyalty program offering personalized experiences and rewards across digital and physical channels.

- Nike App: An app providing personalized product recommendations, exclusive content, and seamless shopping experiences.

- In-Store Technology: Interactive displays and digital touchpoints in stores to enhance the shopping experience.

- Results: Nike's integrated strategy resulted in increased customer engagement, higher sales and improved customer loyalty.

CASE STUDY 2: STARBUCKS

- Objective: Starbucks aimed to enhance customer convenience and drive engagement through digital-physical integration.

- Strategy: Starbucks implemented the following initiatives:

- Mobile App: A mobile app allowing customers to order ahead, pay digitally, and earn rewards.

- In-Store Integration: Digital menu boards, mobile order pickup stations, and personalized in-store experiences.

- Omnichannel Campaigns: Coordinated marketing campaigns across social media, email, and in-store promotions.

- Results: Starbucks achieved higher customer satisfaction, increased mobile app usage and improved sales performance.

CASE STUDY 3: SEPHORA

- Objective: Sephora aimed to create a unified shopping experience that bridges the gap between online and offline channels.

- Strategy: Sephora implemented several initiatives, including:

- Digital Tools: Virtual try-on tools, personalized product recommendations, and an interactive mobile app.

- In-Store Technology: Digital displays, QR codes for product information, and a seamless checkout process.

- Omnichannel Loyalty Program: A loyalty program rewarding customers for both online and in-store purchases.

- Results: Sephora's integrated strategy led to increased customer engagement, higher conversion rates, and enhanced customer loyalty.

CASE STUDY 4: HDFC BANK

- Objective: HDFC Bank aimed to integrate digital and physical banking services to enhance customer convenience and engagement.

- Strategy: HDFC Bank adopted several initiatives, including:

- Digital Banking Platform: A comprehensive digital platform offering online banking services, including account management, bill payments, and loan applications.

- Physical Branch Integration: Enhanced branch experience with digital kiosks and tablets for customer assistance.

- Omnichannel Marketing: Coordinated campaigns across digital platforms, physical branches and ATM locations.

- Results: HDFC Bank's integrated approach resulted in improved customer satisfaction, increased digital banking adoption, and enhanced branch performance.

CASE STUDY 5: RELIANCE JIO

- Objective: Reliance Jio aimed to create a seamless integration between digital and physical retail experiences.

- Strategy: Reliance Jio implemented the following strategies:

- Jio App: A comprehensive app offering services including recharges, customer support, and exclusive offers.

- Physical Store Integration: Stores equipped with digital kiosks for quick service and seamless customer interactions.

- Integrated Promotions: Coordinated marketing campaigns that drive online app downloads and in-store visits.

- Results: Reliance Jio's strategy led to a significant increase in-app usage, higher footfall in stores, and strong customer loyalty.

By studying these successful implementations, you can gain valuable insights into effective strategies and best practices for integrating digital and physical marketing efforts. Adapt these learnings to suit your brand and audience and continuously refine your approach based on performance data and customer feedback.

5

LEVERAGING TECHNOLOGY FOR INTEGRATION

In my journey as a marketer, I've come to appreciate how technology is not just a tool but a catalyst that can transform our approach to integrating digital and physical marketing. Technology's role in bridging these two worlds is profound, enabling us to create more cohesive and engaging experiences for our audiences. Reflecting on my experiences, I am constantly amazed by how innovative tech solutions can enhance and unify marketing strategies.

One of the most compelling aspects of leveraging technology is its ability to gather and analyse data in ways that were once unimaginable. Take, for instance, how Amazon uses its sophisticated algorithms and data analytics to offer personalized shopping experiences. By analyzing customer behavior and preferences, Amazon can seamlessly blend its digital recommendations with physical store experiences, such as its cashier-less Amazon Go stores. This integration exemplifies how technology can transform both online and offline interactions into a unified customer journey.

In the Indian market, brands like HDFC Bank have demonstrated the power of technology in integrating their digital and physical presence. The bank's use of digital platforms to complement its physical branches, such as through mobile banking apps that offer features like branch locator and appointment scheduling, provides a cohesive customer experience. This seamless integration not only enhances convenience, but also strengthens customer loyalty.

Similarly, Nike's use of technology to enhance its brand experience is noteworthy. Nike's "NikeFit" app, which uses augmented reality to help customers find the perfect shoe size, bridges the gap between digital convenience and physical product interaction. This tech-driven solution enhances the in-store experience by providing valuable insights that guide purchasing decisions, thereby creating a more personalized and integrated customer journey.

In the Indian retail space, Future Group's use of technology in their Big Bazaar stores provides an illustrative example. The integration of digital kiosks, loyalty programs, and mobile apps with physical retail operations allows customers to check prices, access promotions, and earn rewards seamlessly. This technological synergy helps bridge the gap between online and offline shopping, delivering a unified and engaging customer experience.

Reflecting on these examples, it's clear that technology is a powerful enabler of integration, transforming how we connect with consumers across digital and physical touchpoints. As we delve into this chapter, I am excited to explore how various technologies can be harnessed to bridge the digital-physical divide, drawing inspiration from both global and Indian success stories. I hope to provide insights that will help you leverage technology effectively to create a more cohesive and impactful marketing strategy.

ESSENTIAL TECHNOLOGIES FOR DIGITAL-PHYSICAL INTEGRATION

To effectively integrate digital and physical marketing efforts, leveraging the right technologies is paramount. These tools facilitate smooth transitions between online and offline experiences, enhance customer engagement, and offer valuable data for informed decision-making. Below are essential technologies detailed with examples from Indian businesses:

1. Customer Relationship Management (CRM) Systems

   - Centralized Customer Data: CRM systems aggregate customer data from all interaction points, offering a comprehensive view of each customer. This data encompasses purchase history, preferences, and interactions across digital and physical channels. For instance, Big Bazaar uses CRM systems to track customer purchase patterns and tailor marketing campaigns based on their buying history.

   - Personalization: CRM data enables personalized marketing efforts by customizing content and offers according to individual customer needs and preferences. HDFC Bank, for example, leverages CRM data to personalize offers and financial products to its customers based on their transaction history and behavior.

2. Marketing Automation Platforms

- Streamlined Campaign Management: Marketing automation platforms simplify the management of marketing campaigns across various channels. These platforms automate tasks such as email marketing, social media posting, and lead nurturing. Zomato employs marketing automation to send personalized offers and reminders to users based on their ordering history and preferences.

- Data Integration: These platforms integrate data from diverse sources, allowing for improved targeting and segmentation. Nykaa, an Indian beauty and wellness retailer, uses marketing automation to synchronize data from its online store, social media, and customer interactions, enabling more precise targeting and personalized promotions.

3. Customer Experience Management (CXM) Solutions

- Real-Time Insights: CXM solutions deliver real-time insights into customer interactions and experiences across all touchpoints, helping to pinpoint areas for improvement and optimize customer engagement. Flipkart utilizes CXM solutions to monitor customer feedback and improve service quality across its e-commerce platform.

- Personalized Engagement: CXM tools facilitate personalized experiences based on customer behavior and preferences. Jabong, an online fashion retailer, uses CXM to provide tailored shopping experiences by analyzing customer behavior and purchase history.

4. Point-of-Sale (POS) Systems

- Unified Transactions: Integrating POS systems with digital platforms ensures seamless transitions between online and offline transactions. Features such as online order pickup, in-store inventory checks, and unified customer profiles are supported. Shoppers Stop integrates its POS system with its online platform to offer features like 'Click and Collect', where customers can order items online and pick them up at the store.

- Data Collection: POS systems collect data from in-store transactions to enhance customer profiles and refine marketing strategies. Reliance Fresh uses POS data to track sales trends and customer preferences, which informs inventory management and promotional strategies.

5. Analytics and Data Visualization Tools

- Performance Tracking: Analytics tools help track the performance of marketing efforts across channels. Key metrics, such as customer acquisition cost, conversion rates, and customer lifetime value, can be monitored. Tata Motors employs analytics tools to track the effectiveness of its marketing campaigns and customer engagement across various platforms.

- Data Visualization: Data visualization tools aid in identifying trends and insights, simplifying data interpretation, and decision-making. Café Coffee Day (CCD) uses data visualization to analyze sales trends and customer preferences, which helps in strategizing marketing and product offerings.

6. Content Management Systems (CMS)

- Consistent Content Delivery: A CMS helps manage and distribute content consistently across all channels, ensuring cohesive and up-to-date brand messaging. Saree.com, an online saree retailer, uses a CMS to maintain consistent product information and promotions across its website and mobile app.

- Content Adaptation: Adapt content for different channels, optimizing it for both digital and physical touchpoints. Haldiram's adapts its content and promotions for both its online presence and physical stores to maintain a cohesive brand experience.

IMPLEMENTING AND INTEGRATING TECHNOLOGY SOLUTIONS

Successfully implementing and integrating technology solutions requires a strategic approach. Here are the detailed steps:

1. Assessment and Planning

    - Needs Analysis: Conduct a comprehensive needs analysis to determine the technologies necessary for digital-physical integration. Consider marketing goals, target audience, and existing infrastructure. Marico, for example, assessed its digital and physical needs to implement an integrated marketing strategy for its personal care products.

    - Vendor Selection: Evaluate and choose vendors offering the best solutions. Consider features, scalability, ease of integration, and cost. Godrej, for instance, carefully selected vendors for its CRM and marketing automation needs to enhance its customer engagement efforts.

2. System Integration

    - Data Integration: Ensure all technology solutions are integrated to allow seamless data flow between systems. This might involve integrating CRM, marketing automation, POS, and analytics platforms. Aditya Birla Group integrates its various systems to ensure a unified customer experience across its diverse portfolio of brands.

    - APIs and Middleware: Utilize APIs and middleware to facilitate system integration, ensuring synchronized and accessible data across platforms. HDFC Life uses APIs to connect its CRM, digital platforms, and customer service systems for a seamless experience.

3. Implementation

- Phased Approach: Implement technology solutions in phases to manage complexity and reduce disruption. Start with core systems and gradually integrate additional tools. Oyo Rooms phased its technology upgrades to ensure smooth transitions and minimize operational disruptions.

- Testing: Perform thorough testing to confirm that systems function correctly and data flows seamlessly. Address issues before full deployment. ICICI Bank conducts extensive testing of its digital banking systems to ensure reliability and user satisfaction.

4. Training and Adoption

- Employee Training: Provide training on new technology solutions to ensure proper usage and adoption. Offer comprehensive training sessions and ongoing support. Wipro invests in training its employees on new digital tools and systems to ensure effective use and integration.

- Change Management: Implement change management strategies to help employees adapt to new systems. Communicate benefits and provide resources for a smooth transition. Infosys employs change management strategies to facilitate the adoption of new technologies within the organization.

5. Ongoing Maintenance and Optimization

- Regular Updates: Keep technology solutions current with regular updates and patches to ensure security and optimal performance. Cognizant regularly updates its technology systems to maintain security and functionality.

- Performance Monitoring: Continuously monitor technology performance using analytics to track usage, identify issues, and optimize processes. Tech Mahindra uses performance monitoring tools to track and enhance the performance of its digital solutions.

- Feedback Loop: Establish feedback mechanisms with employees and customers to gather insights and identify areas for improvement. Use feedback to refine and enhance technology solutions. Bharat Petroleum uses customer feedback to improve its digital services and customer engagement strategies.

BEST PRACTICES FOR SEAMLESS INTEGRATION

To achieve seamless integration of digital and physical marketing efforts, adhere to the following best practices:

1. Unified Data Strategy

- Data Consistency: Ensure data consistency across all systems and touchpoints by standardizing formats and ensuring accurate data entry. HCL Technologies ensures data consistency across its platforms for coherent customer insights and marketing strategies.

- Single Customer View: Strive to create a unified view of the customer by consolidating data from all sources. This enhances targeting and personalization. Spencer's Retail consolidates data from online and offline sources to provide a holistic view of customer behavior.

2. Cross-Channel Coordination

- Integrated Campaigns: Plan and execute campaigns that leverage both digital and physical channels. Ensure coordinated messaging, timing, and offers across channels. Bata India integrates its digital and physical marketing campaigns to ensure a consistent brand message and customer experience.

- Omnichannel Experience: Provide a seamless omnichannel experience by allowing customers to transition effortlessly between online and offline touchpoints. For instance, Lenskart offers online order and in-store pickup options, creating a smooth omnichannel experience.

3. Personalization at Scale

- Data-Driven Personalization: Use data to personalize marketing efforts at scale, tailoring content, offers, and recommendations based on customer behavior and preferences. BookMyShow uses data-driven personalization to recommend events and movie showtimes based on user interests.

- Automation: Utilize marketing automation tools to deliver personalized experiences efficiently. Automate tasks such as email marketing, lead nurturing, and customer segmentation. Jabong uses automation to provide personalized fashion recommendations and offers based on user behavior.

4. Customer-Centric Approach

- Customer Feedback: Collect and analyse customer feedback to identify areas for improvement. Use this feedback to inform marketing strategies and enhance the customer experience. HDFC Life gathers feedback to refine its insurance products and services.

- Customer Journey Mapping: Map the customer journey to identify key touchpoints and opportunities for personalization. Ensure each interaction contributes to a cohesive and enjoyable experience. Titan Watches maps the customer journey to personalize interactions and enhance the shopping experience.

5. Continuous Improvement

- Performance Monitoring: Regularly monitor marketing performance across channels. Use analytics to track key metrics and identify trends. HCL Technologies tracks performance metrics to continuously refine its marketing strategies.

- Iterative Approach: Adopt an iterative approach to marketing by continuously refining strategies based on performance data and customer feedback. Conduct A/B testing to identify the most effective tactics. HDFC Bank uses A/B testing to optimize its digital campaigns and enhance customer engagement.

By leveraging the right technologies and adhering to best practices for integration, you can create a seamless and engaging customer experience that bridges the gap between digital and physical marketing efforts. This approach not only enhances customer satisfaction, but also drives long-term business success.

6

CRAFTING COHESIVE CUSTOMER EXPERIENCES

As a marketer deeply invested in creating memorable and impactful interactions, I've come to recognize that crafting cohesive customer experiences is the cornerstone of effective marketing. It's not just about delivering a message; it's about weaving a seamless narrative that guides customers through every touchpoint—whether digital or physical. This approach ensures that every interaction feels connected and meaningful, ultimately fostering stronger brand loyalty and engagement.

Reflecting on my experiences, one of the most profound lessons I've learned is that a cohesive customer experience goes beyond consistent messaging. It requires a holistic understanding of the customer journey and the ability to integrate various channels and touchpoints into a unified experience. This integration is crucial for creating a sense of continuity and ensuring that customers feel valued and understood throughout their interaction with the brand.

A prime example of this is Apple. The company excels at creating a seamless customer experience by integrating its products, services, and retail environments. From the intuitive user interface of its devices to the seamless interaction between its digital services and physical Apple Stores, Apple demonstrates how a cohesive experience can enhance customer satisfaction and loyalty. The in-store experience is meticulously designed to complement the online ecosystem, creating a unified brand presence that resonates with customers on multiple levels.

In the Indian market, brands like Tata Motors offer a compelling example of crafting cohesive customer experiences. Tata Motors integrates its digital presence with its physical showrooms by offering features such as virtual car tours and online booking options, supported by an immersive in-store experience. This approach ensures that customers transitioning from online research to a physical showroom encounter a seamless and consistent experience, reinforcing their engagement with the brand.

Similarly, Starbucks' approach to creating a cohesive experience is noteworthy. The company's use of its mobile app to enhance the in-store experience is a testament to its commitment to customer satisfaction. The app not only allows for convenient ordering and payment, but also integrates with the physical store environment through features like in-store pickup and personalized offers. This seamless integration enhances the overall customer journey, creating a more engaging and satisfying experience.

In the Indian retail sector, Nykaa's omnichannel strategy illustrates the power of a cohesive customer experience. By integrating its online platform with its physical stores, Nykaa ensures that customers enjoy a consistent experience, whether they're shopping online or in-store. Features such as online product availability checks, in-store pickup options, and personalized recommendations create a unified experience that meets the needs of modern consumers.

As we explore the concepts and strategies in this chapter, I hope to share insights on how to craft cohesive customer experiences that blend digital and physical touchpoints seamlessly. By drawing from both global and Indian examples, I aim to provide a comprehensive understanding of how to create experiences that not only meet, but exceed, customer expectations, ultimately driving brand loyalty and success.

UNDERSTANDING CUSTOMER TOUCHPOINTS

Creating a cohesive customer experience necessitates a thorough understanding of the diverse touchpoints where customers engage with your brand. These touchpoints are broadly categorized into digital and physical interactions. Here's an in-depth overview:

1. Digital Touchpoints

    - Website: Your website often serves as the primary point of contact for customers. It should be user-friendly, visually appealing, and in alignment with your brand's identity and messaging. For instance, Flipkart ensures its website is easy to navigate, offers detailed product descriptions, and integrates user reviews to enhance the customer experience.

- Social Media: Platforms such as Facebook, Instagram, Twitter, and LinkedIn offer valuable opportunities for engagement, content sharing, and customer service. Jabong actively engages with customers through social media, running campaigns, responding to queries, and sharing user-generated content.

- Email Marketing: Personalized email campaigns can nurture leads, update customers about new products and drive sales. Nykaa uses email marketing to inform customers about beauty trends, exclusive offers, and personalized product recommendations.

- Online Ads: Digital advertisements, including display ads, search ads, and social media ads, help attract potential customers and drive traffic to your website. Myntra utilizes online ads to promote seasonal sales and exclusive collections, driving both online traffic and in-store visits.

- Mobile Apps: Mobile apps provide personalized experiences, push notifications, and convenient shopping options. Big Bazaar's app offers features like personalized discounts, in-app ordering, and loyalty rewards, enhancing the overall customer experience.

2. Physical Touchpoints

- Retail Stores: Brick-and-mortar stores offer a tangible experience where customers can physically interact with products and receive face-to-face assistance. Shoppers Stop creates immersive in-store experiences with well-trained staff and interactive displays.

- Events and Trade Shows: These venues provide opportunities for direct engagement, product demonstrations, and networking. Titan regularly participates in trade shows to showcase new watch collections and engage with potential customers.

- Printed Materials: Brochures, catalogs, and direct mail complement digital efforts and provide additional information. Haldiram's uses printed materials in-store to highlight new products and special offers, bridging the gap between digital marketing and physical retail.

- Customer Service: In-person customer service interactions significantly impact the overall customer experience. Reliance Fresh ensures its staff provides excellent service, assisting customers with their queries and enhancing their shopping experience.

CREATING SEAMLESS TRANSITIONS BETWEEN DIGITAL AND PHYSICAL CHANNELS

To provide a cohesive customer experience, it's crucial to create smooth transitions between digital and physical channels. Here are strategies to achieve this:

1. Unified Branding and Messaging

    - Consistent Visual Identity: Maintain consistent branding elements such as logos, colors, fonts, and imagery across all touchpoints. This consistency strengthens brand recognition and trust. Patanjali Ayurved ensures its visual identity remains cohesive across its website, social media, and retail packaging.

    - Aligned Messaging: Ensure that messaging is consistent across all channels. Key messages, taglines, and tone of voice should be uniform, whether in an email, social media post, or in-store signage. Café Coffee Day aligns its messaging across its app, website, and in-store promotions to reinforce brand identity.

2. Integrated Customer Data

    - Centralized Data Collection: Collect and store customer data from all touchpoints in a centralized system, such as a CRM. This creates a single view of the customer and allows for more effective personalization. HDFC Bank centralizes data from online banking, mobile apps, and branch interactions to tailor services and offers.

- Data Sharing: Ensure customer data is accessible to all relevant departments. For example, in-store staff should have access to a customer's online purchase history to provide more informed service. Godrej Appliances integrates data from its e-commerce platform with in-store systems to offer personalized customer support.

3. Omnichannel Strategies

- Unified Commerce: Allow customers to transition seamlessly between online and offline channels. For example, enable online purchases with in-store pickup or returns. Lenskart offers options to buy glasses online and try them at home, or pick them up at a physical store.

- Cross-Channel Promotions: Run promotions valid across all channels. For instance, offer a discount code redeemable both online and in-store. Spencer's Retail runs cross-channel promotions that customers can use both online and at physical stores, ensuring a consistent shopping experience.

- Consistent Customer Support: Provide uniform customer support across channels. Whether customers contact you via social media, email, or in-store, they should receive the same quality of service. Tata Motors ensures its customer support is consistent across its website, service centers, and social media channels.

4. Personalized Experiences

- Tailored Recommendations: Use data from past interactions to offer personalized recommendations. For instance, suggest products based on previous purchases or browsing history. Amazon India uses advanced algorithms to provide personalized product recommendations based on user behavior.

- Targeted Campaigns: Run targeted marketing campaigns based on customer segmentation. Tailor content and offers to meet the specific needs and preferences of each segment. Marico uses segmentation to target different consumer groups with personalized offers and campaigns for its health and beauty products.

- Behavioral Triggers: Employ triggers based on customer behavior to deliver personalized experiences. For example, send follow-up emails if a customer abandons their online cart or provide in-store assistance if they linger in a specific section. Nykaa sends reminders and personalized offers to customers who have items in their cart but haven't completed the purchase.

DESIGNING CUSTOMER JOURNEYS

Designing effective customer journeys involves mapping out the steps a customer takes from awareness to purchase and beyond. Here's how to create a comprehensive customer journey map:

1. Identify Stages of the Journey

    - Awareness: The customer becomes aware of your brand through advertising, social media, word-of-mouth, etc. Bata India increases brand awareness through various advertising channels, social media campaigns and influencer partnerships.

    - Consideration: The customer researches and evaluates your products or services, comparing them with competitors. Parle-G provides detailed product information and consumer reviews to assist customers in their consideration phase.

    - Purchase: The customer completes a purchase, either online or in-store. Reliance Digital offers a smooth purchase experience, both online and offline, with options for home delivery or in-store pickup.

    - Post-Purchase: The customer uses the product, seeks support if needed, and may provide feedback or reviews. HDFC Life follows up with customers post-purchase to offer support and gather feedback on their insurance products.

    - Loyalty: The customer becomes loyal to your brand, making repeat purchases and recommending your products to others. Saree.com incentivizes repeat purchases with loyalty programmes and referral rewards.

2. Map Out Touchpoints

    - List All Touchpoints: Identify every touchpoint a customer interacts with at each stage of their journey. Include both digital and physical interactions. Oyo Rooms maps out touchpoints such as app interactions, website visits, customer service calls, and hotel stays.

- Sequence of Interactions: Determine the typical sequence of interactions. For example, a customer might see an online ad, visit your website, read reviews, and then visit a store. Dabur tracks customer journeys from online research to in-store purchase, and post-purchase feedback.

3. Analyse Customer Behavior

- Behavioral Data: Utilize data analytics to understand how customers move through their journey. Identify common paths and obstacles. Flipkart analyses user behavior to optimize its website navigation and streamline the checkout process.

- Feedback and Surveys: Collect feedback through surveys and customer interviews to gain insights into their experiences and pain points. Lenskart uses customer feedback to refine its product offerings and improve the shopping experience.

4. Optimize the Journey

- Eliminate Friction: Identify and address friction points in the journey. For example, streamline the checkout process or enhance website navigation. Jabong improved its checkout process by simplifying steps and reducing cart abandonment rates.

- Enhance Engagement: Use personalized content and offers to enhance engagement at each stage. For example, send personalized emails during the consideration phase or offer loyalty rewards post-purchase. Nykaa sends personalized beauty recommendations and exclusive offers based on customer preferences.

- Monitor and Iterate: Continuously monitor the customer journey and make iterative improvements based on data and feedback. HDFC Bank regularly reviews customer journey data to refine its digital banking services and enhance customer satisfaction.

CASE STUDIES: EXEMPLARY CUSTOMER EXPERIENCES

Examining real-world examples of brands that have successfully created cohesive customer experiences provides valuable insights and inspiration. Here are several case studies:

CASE STUDY 1: APPLE

- Unified Ecosystem: Apple delivers a seamless experience across its ecosystem of products and services. Customers can begin a task on one device and continue it on another without interruption, ensuring a smooth user experience.

- In-Store Experience: Apple Stores offer a high-touch experience with knowledgeable staff, hands-on product demos, and educational workshops. The in-store experience complements the online ecosystem.

- Integrated Support: Apple Support is accessible through multiple channels, including in-store, online, and via the Apple Support app, providing consistent and efficient assistance.

CASE STUDY 2: WARBY PARKER

- Online and Offline Integration: Warby Parker effectively integrates its online and offline channels. Customers can order glasses online to try on.

  at home or visit a physical store for an eye exam and fitting, creating a flexible shopping experience.

  - Consistent Branding: The brand maintains uniform messaging and visual identity across its website, mobile app, and physical stores, reinforcing brand coherence.

  - Customer-Centric Approach: Warby Parker values customer feedback and continuously iterates on its products and services based on consumer insights, demonstrating its commitment to customer satisfaction.

CASE STUDY 3: DISNEY

- Omnichannel Experience: Disney provides a cohesive experience across its parks, resorts and digital platforms. The My Disney Experience app allows guests to plan their visit, make reservations and access digital tickets, integrating various touchpoints.

- Personalization: Disney uses data to personalize guest experiences, suggesting attractions and dining options based on individual preferences and past behavior, enhancing the overall visit.

- Engaging Content: Disney engages customers with captivating storytelling across movies, TV shows, social media, and in-park experiences, maintaining a strong and consistent brand narrative.

CASE STUDY 4: ZOMATO

- Digital and Physical Integration: Zomato effectively integrates its app with physical dining experiences. Users can browse restaurant reviews, make reservations, and receive personalized recommendations based on their dining history.

- Consistent Branding: Zomato maintains a consistent visual identity and messaging across its app, website, and marketing materials, ensuring a unified brand presence.

- Customer Feedback: Zomato actively seeks and incorporates customer feedback, continuously refining its platform and services based on user experiences and suggestions.

By analyzing these examples, you can gain valuable insights into creating cohesive customer experiences that integrate digital and physical channels effectively. Adapt these best practices to fit your brand and audience, and continuously refine your approach based on performance data and customer feedback.

7

MEASURING SUCCESS AND ROI

In the world of marketing, one of the most crucial aspects of any campaign is understanding its impact and effectiveness. As a marketer, I've learned that measuring success and ROI (Return on Investment) is not just about evaluating numbers; it's about translating those numbers into actionable insights that drive strategic decisions and future innovations. Reflecting on my experiences, I've come to appreciate the complexity and importance of quantifying the success of our efforts in both digital and physical marketing realms.

One of the key realizations in my journey has been that measuring success goes beyond tracking basic metrics. It involves a deeper understanding of how various marketing activities contribute to overall business goals and how they intersect to create value. For instance, the challenge often lies in connecting the dots between digital engagement and physical outcomes, ensuring that every touchpoint is accounted for in the ROI calculation.

A powerful example of this is Coca-Cola's approach to measuring the success of its global campaigns. Coca-Cola uses a combination of digital analytics, sales data and consumer feedback to assess the effectiveness of its marketing strategies. By integrating data from various sources, Coca-Cola can gain a comprehensive view of its campaign performance, allowing for more informed decision-making and optimization.

In the Indian market, brands like HDFC Life Insurance showcase an advanced approach to measuring ROI. HDFC Life leverages sophisticated analytics tools to track the performance of its marketing campaigns across different channels. By analyzing data from online and offline interactions, HDFC Life can evaluate the impact of its efforts on lead generation and customer acquisition, ensuring that marketing investments are aligned with business objectives.

Similarly, Amazon India exemplifies the importance of measuring success through data-driven insights. The company utilizes an array of metrics, from website traffic and conversion rates to customer reviews and return rates, to evaluate the performance of its marketing initiatives. This comprehensive approach allows Amazon India to optimize its campaigns and enhance customer experiences, ultimately driving greater ROI.

Another notable example is the Indian retail brand Reliance Trends, which integrates data from both online and physical stores to assess the success of its marketing strategies. By tracking metrics such as in-store foot traffic, online engagement, and sales conversions, Reliance Trends can gain a holistic view of its campaign effectiveness and make data-driven decisions to improve its marketing efforts.

As we delve into this chapter, I am excited to explore the various methodologies and tools available for measuring success and ROI. By drawing insights from both international and Indian brand examples, I aim to provide a comprehensive understanding of how to effectively evaluate marketing performance and ensure that every investment contributes to achieving strategic goals. Measuring success and ROI is not just about numbers; it's about leveraging those numbers to drive growth and create lasting impact.

KEY METRICS FOR DIGITAL-PHYSICAL INTEGRATION

Measuring the success of integrated marketing strategies requires a comprehensive understanding of various metrics that span both digital and physical channels. Here's a deeper dive into key performance indicators (KPIs) essential for evaluating your marketing efforts:

1. Customer Acquisition Cost (CAC)

   - Definition: CAC represents the total expense involved in acquiring a new customer, encompassing all marketing and sales-related costs.

   - Calculation: CAC is calculated by dividing the total cost of marketing and sales by the number of new customers acquired in a given period.

   - Importance: Monitoring CAC helps in evaluating the cost-effectiveness of your marketing strategies and understanding the financial efficiency of acquiring new customers. High CAC may indicate inefficiencies in your marketing approach or sales process, while a low CAC suggests a more efficient customer acquisition strategy.

2. Customer Lifetime Value (CLV)

- Definition: CLV estimates the total revenue a business can expect from a customer throughout their relationship with the brand.

- Calculation: CLV is calculated by multiplying the average purchase value by the average purchase frequency, and then by the average customer lifespan.

- Importance: CLV provides insights into the long-term value and profitability of customers, guiding marketing investment decisions and strategies for customer retention. By increasing CLV, businesses can focus on retaining customers and encouraging repeat purchases, which can be more cost-effective than acquiring new customers.

3. Conversion Rate

- Definition: The conversion rate measures the percentage of visitors who complete a desired action, such as making a purchase or subscribing to a newsletter.

- Calculation: It is determined by dividing the number of conversions by the total number of visitors and multiplying by 100.

- Importance: This metric gauges the effectiveness of marketing campaigns in driving user actions. A high conversion rate indicates that your marketing efforts are successful in compelling customers to engage, while a low rate may suggest the need for campaign optimization or adjustments to your sales funnel.

4. Return on Investment (ROI)

- Definition: ROI measures the profitability of marketing investments by comparing revenue generated from marketing activities to the costs incurred.

- Calculation: ROI is calculated using the formula: (Revenue Generated from Marketing - Marketing Costs) / Marketing Costs x 100.

- Importance: ROI provides a clear picture of the financial return on marketing expenditures. Positive ROI indicates effective use of marketing resources, while negative ROI signals the need for strategic reassessment.

5. Customer Retention Rate

- Definition: This metric tracks the percentage of customers who continue to purchase from your brand over a specific period.

- Calculation: It is calculated by taking the number of customers at the end of a period, subtracting the number of new customers acquired during that period, dividing by the number of customers at the start of the period, and then multiplying by 100.

- Importance: Retention rate highlights customer loyalty and the effectiveness of your retention strategies. A high retention rate indicates satisfied customers and successful engagement strategies, while a low rate suggests that improvements are needed in customer service or relationship management.

6. Engagement Metrics

- Definition: Engagement metrics measure the level of interaction customers have with your brand across various touchpoints.

- Examples: These include social media likes, shares, comments, email open rates, click-through rates, and website dwell time.

- Importance: Engagement metrics offer insights into how well your content resonates with your audience and the effectiveness of your marketing efforts. High engagement levels often correlate with increased brand awareness and customer loyalty.

TOOLS FOR TRACKING AND ANALYZING PERFORMANCE

To accurately track and analyse the performance of your integrated marketing efforts, utilize the following tools:

1. Google Analytics

    - Features: Google Analytics provides comprehensive insights into website traffic, user behavior and conversion tracking.

    - Use Case: This tool is instrumental in monitoring digital campaign performance, understanding customer journeys, and evaluating website effectiveness. By setting up goals and tracking metrics, such as bounce rates and session duration, businesses can gain valuable insights into user behavior and campaign success.

2. Customer Relationship Management (CRM) Systems

    - Features: CRM systems centralize customer data, track interactions across touchpoints and offer insights into customer behavior and preferences.

    - Use Case: CRMs are vital for managing customer relationships, segmenting audiences, and personalizing marketing efforts. By integrating CRM data with marketing automation tools, businesses can enhance their targeting and communication strategies, leading to improved customer engagement and retention.

3. Marketing Automation Platforms

    - Features: These platforms automate marketing tasks, track campaign performance, and provide analytics on email marketing, social media, and other channels.

- Use Case: Marketing automation tools streamline operations, measure campaign effectiveness and optimize customer engagement. They enable businesses to execute targeted campaigns, track performance metrics and refine strategies based on real-time data.

4. Point-of-Sale (POS) Systems

- Features: POS systems track in-store sales, integrate with inventory management, and collect customer data at the point of purchase.

- Use Case: POS systems are crucial for measuring physical retail performance, tracking sales data and integrating with digital systems for a unified view of customer interactions. They provide insights into purchase patterns and inventory management, supporting data-driven decision-making.

5. Social Media Analytics Tools

- Features: These tools analyse social media performance, track engagement metrics, and monitor brand sentiment.

- Use Case: Social media analytics tools help measure the impact of social media campaigns, track audience engagement, and gather insights for content optimization. By understanding social media performance, businesses can adjust their strategies to better align with audience preferences.

6. A/B Testing Tools

    - Features: A/B testing tools allow businesses to test different variations of marketing campaigns to determine which performs better.

    - Use Case: A/B testing is essential for optimizing marketing efforts by comparing variables such as email subject lines, ad creatives, and website layouts. By analyzing the results of different variations, businesses can refine their marketing strategies for maximum effectiveness.

ESTABLISHING A FEEDBACK LOOP

To continuously improve your integrated marketing efforts, establish a feedback loop involving the collection, analysis and action of data. Here's a detailed approach:

1. Data Collection

    - Surveys and Feedback Forms: Utilize surveys and feedback forms to obtain direct input from customers about their experiences and preferences. This method provides qualitative insights into customer satisfaction and areas for improvement.

    - Customer Interactions: Gather data from customer interactions across all touchpoints, including online and in-store. This comprehensive data collection helps in understanding customer behavior and engagement levels.

    - Behavioral Data: Track customer behavior using analytics tools to gain insights into how customers engage with your brand. This data helps identify trends and patterns in customer interactions and preferences.

2. Data Analysis

- Identify Trends: Analyse collected data to identify trends, patterns, and insights. Look for areas where your marketing efforts are successful, and areas needing improvement. Data analysis helps in understanding the effectiveness of your strategies and making informed decisions.

- Segment Analysis: Segment your audience to understand the behavior and preferences of different customer groups. Tailoring marketing strategies to specific segments can enhance engagement and drive better results.

3. Actionable Insights

- Optimize Campaigns: Use insights gained from data analysis to optimize marketing campaigns. Adjust strategies based on performance data to improve effectiveness and achieve better results.

- Personalization: Personalize marketing efforts based on customer preferences and behavior. Deliver relevant content and offers to enhance engagement and build stronger customer relationships.

4. Continuous Improvement

   - Regular Review: Regularly review marketing performance and adjust strategies accordingly. Periodic reviews ensure that you stay on track and make necessary changes based on performance data.

   - Iterative Approach: Adopt an iterative approach to marketing, continuously testing and refining tactics. Use A/B testing to identify the most effective strategies and make data-driven decisions.

CASE STUDIES: MEASURING SUCCESS AND ROI

Examining real-world examples of brands that have successfully measured and optimized their integrated marketing efforts can provide valuable insights. Here are a few case studies:

CASE STUDY 1: AMAZON.

- Metrics Tracked: Amazon tracks metrics such as customer acquisition cost, customer lifetime value, and engagement metrics.

- Tools Used: Amazon utilizes advanced analytics platforms, CRM systems, and A/B testing tools to measure and optimize marketing performance.

- Results: Amazon's data-driven approach enables continuous optimization of marketing efforts. They leverage customer behavior data to personalize recommendations, resulting in higher conversion rates and customer loyalty.

CASE STUDY 2: COCA-COLA

- Metrics Tracked: Coca-Cola tracks brand awareness, customer engagement, and sales data to measure the impact of marketing campaigns.

- Tools Used: Coca-Cola integrates data from social media analytics tools, CRM systems, and POS systems.

- Results: By combining insights from various sources, Coca-Cola creates cohesive marketing campaigns that drive brand engagement and increase sales. Their integrated approach ensures a unified brand experience across digital and physical channels.

CASE STUDY 3: SEPHORA

- Metrics Tracked: Sephora monitors metrics such as customer retention rate, conversion rate, and customer lifetime value.

- Tools Used: Sephora employs CRM systems, marketing automation platforms, and POS systems to manage and analyse customer data.

- Results: Sephora's integrated marketing strategy delivers personalized experiences across online and offline channels. By tracking customer interactions and preferences, Sephora enhances customer satisfaction, driving loyalty.

CASE STUDY 4: BIG BAZAAR

- Metrics Tracked: Big Bazaar focuses on metrics like foot traffic, sales conversion rates, and customer satisfaction scores.

- Tools Used: The retail giant uses POS systems, social media analytics, and customer feedback surveys.

- Results: Big Bazaar leverages these metrics to optimize in-store promotions and digital marketing efforts.

The integration of data from both online and offline sources helps them enhance the shopping experience and boost sales.

CASE STUDY 5: NYKAA

- Metrics Tracked: Nykaa tracks customer acquisition cost, customer lifetime value, and online engagement metrics.

- Tools Used: Nykaa utilizes CRM systems, marketing automation platforms and social media analytics tools.

- Results: Nykaa's focus on integrating digital and physical marketing efforts has led to a successful omnichannel strategy. By analyzing customer data, Nykaa personalises offers and enhances the shopping experience, resulting in increased customer retention and revenue.

By studying these examples, you can gain valuable insights into effective strategies for measuring success and ROI in integrated marketing. Adapt these best practices to your brand's unique needs, and continuously refine your approach based on performance data and customer feedback.

<h1 style="text-align:center">8</h1>

OVERCOMING CHALLENGES IN DIGITAL-PHYSICAL INTEGRATION

I've encountered numerous challenges that have shaped my understanding of this complex yet rewarding field. The journey of bridging the digital-physical divide is both exhilarating and demanding, filled with obstacles that require innovative solutions and strategic thinking. Reflecting on my experiences, I've learned that overcoming these challenges is crucial for creating a unified and impactful customer experience.

One of the most significant lessons I've learned is that integrating digital and physical marketing requires a keen awareness of the unique challenges each domain presents. It's not simply about merging two different strategies, but about understanding how they can complement each other to enhance the overall customer journey. The road to successful integration is often paved with issues related to data synchronization, consistency in messaging, and technology adoption.

A poignant example of overcoming integration challenges comes from Starbucks. The company has successfully navigated the complexities of integrating its digital loyalty program with its physical store operations. By using data analytics to align digital rewards with in-store promotions, Starbucks has managed to create a seamless experience that encourages customer engagement both online and offline. This integration not only boosts customer satisfaction but also drives repeat business, illustrating the power of overcoming integration hurdles with innovative solutions.

In the Indian context, brands like Reliance Jio have demonstrated remarkable success in tackling integration challenges. Reliance Jio's ability to synchronize its digital offerings, such as its app and online services, with its physical retail presence, has been pivotal in delivering a cohesive customer experience. By addressing challenges related to data integration and consistency, Reliance Jio has set a benchmark for effective digital-physical integration in the Indian market.

Another notable example is the fashion retailer Myntra. Myntra's strategy of integrating its online platform with offline experiences, such as pop-up stores and experiential events, showcases how overcoming integration challenges can lead to innovative marketing approaches. By addressing issues related to inventory management and customer data synchronization, Myntra has managed to offer a cohesive shopping experience that bridges the gap between digital and physical touchpoints.

Internationally, Nike's approach to integrating its digital and physical experiences provides valuable insights. Nike's use of its "Nike+" app to enhance in-store experiences, combined with its digital marketing campaigns, illustrates how overcoming integration challenges can lead to a more personalized and engaging customer journey. Nike's ability to address issues related to technology adoption and data consistency has been key to its success in creating a unified brand experience.

As we dive into this chapter, I am eager to share strategies and insights on overcoming the challenges of digital-physical integration. By drawing from both global and Indian brand examples, I hope to provide practical solutions and innovative approaches that can help marketers navigate the complexities of integrating these two crucial marketing domains. The journey may be fraught with challenges, but with the right strategies, it's possible to transform these obstacles into opportunities for creating a truly cohesive and impactful customer experience.

IDENTIFYING COMMON CHALLENGES

Integrating digital and physical marketing strategies is a complex task that presents numerous challenges. Understanding these obstacles is crucial for devising effective solutions. Here are some expanded insights into common challenges faced during integration:

1. Data Silos

- Description: Data silos occur when information is isolated within different systems or departments, preventing a holistic view of the customer journey.

- Impact: The presence of data silos hampers the ability to deliver personalized experiences and can lead to fragmented customer insights, which affects decision-making and strategy formulation.

  Indian Example: In India, many traditional retail chains face this issue due to legacy systems. For instance, the large retail group Future Group struggled with data silos across its multiple brands. The lack of integration between online and offline sales data made it challenging to offer personalized promotions and track customer behavior effectively.

2. Technological Integration

- Description: This challenge involves the difficulty of integrating various technology platforms and systems, such as CRM, ERP, and marketing automation tools.

- Impact: Poor integration can result in inefficiencies, data inconsistencies, and increased operational costs. It also limits the ability to create a unified customer experience.

  Indian Example: Flipkart, one of India's leading e-commerce platforms, faced technological integration issues when it attempted to merge its diverse technological systems post-acquisition of Myntra. Aligning different tech stacks proved challenging and required significant investment in harmonizing their systems for a seamless customer experience.

3.   Consistency Across Channels

- Description: Maintaining consistent branding, messaging, and customer experience across all digital and physical touchpoints can be challenging.

- Impact: Inconsistencies can confuse customers, erode trust and dilute the brand identity, ultimately affecting customer loyalty and brand perception.

  Indian Example: The Indian luxury fashion retailer, Hidesign, encountered difficulties in ensuring consistency between their online store and physical retail locations. Discrepancies in product availability and pricing between online and offline channels led to customer dissatisfaction and brand confusion.

4.   Resource Allocation

- Description: Balancing budget and resources between digital and physical marketing efforts can be a significant challenge.

- Impact: Misallocation of resources can lead to underperforming campaigns and missed opportunities. It is crucial to allocate resources effectively to optimize the impact of marketing activities.

Indian Example: Pantaloon Retail India Limited faced challenges in balancing its marketing budget between traditional media and digital platforms. Initially, the company allocated a disproportionate amount of its budget to offline channels, missing out on the growing digital audience. They eventually recalibrated their strategy to balance investments across both channels.

5. Customer Privacy and Data Security

- Description: Protecting customer data while complying with privacy regulations is a major concern in digital-physical integration.

- Impact: Data breaches and non-compliance with privacy regulations can damage a company's reputation and lead to legal penalties, affecting customer trust and loyalty.

    Indian Example: The Indian financial services company Paytm faced a significant data security breach that exposed customer information. This incident highlighted the need for stringent data protection measures and compliance with regulations, like the Personal Data Protection Bill in India.

6. Measuring ROI

- Description: Accurately measuring the return on investment (ROI) for integrated marketing campaigns can be complex.

- Impact: Difficulty in tracking ROI can hinder the ability to justify marketing expenditures and optimize strategies. Effective measurement is essential for understanding the impact of marketing activities on business outcomes.

Indian Example: Zomato, the Indian food delivery giant, faced challenges in measuring the ROI of its integrated marketing campaigns due to the complexity of tracking customer interactions across multiple platforms. They had to invest in advanced analytics tools to better understand the impact of their campaigns on user engagement and revenue.

STRATEGIES FOR OVERCOMING CHALLENGES

Addressing the challenges of integrating digital and physical marketing requires strategic approaches. Here are some detailed strategies to overcome these obstacles:

1. Breaking Down Data Silos

   - Centralized Data Systems: Implement a centralized data system, such as a comprehensive CRM, that consolidates data from all touchpoints to provide a unified view of the customer.

   - Data Integration Tools: Utilize data integration tools and middleware to facilitate seamless data flow between disparate systems. Tools like Talend and MuleSoft can help bridge data gaps.

   - Cross-Department Collaboration: Encourage collaboration between different departments to share data and insights. Regular inter-departmental meetings and integrated platforms can help align efforts.

Indian Example: Tata Consultancy Services (TCS) successfully implemented a unified CRM system to integrate data from various client touchpoints. This approach allowed them to provide a cohesive customer experience and enhanced data-driven decision-making.

2. Ensuring Technological Integration

- Scalable Platforms: Invest in scalable technology platforms that can integrate with existing systems and accommodate future growth. Platforms, such as Salesforce or Microsoft Dynamics, offer flexibility and scalability.

- API-Driven Integration: Leverage APIs (Application Programming Interfaces) to connect different systems and facilitate data exchange. APIs enable seamless integration and real-time data synchronization.

- Regular Audits: Conduct regular audits of your technology stack to identify and address integration issues. Continuous monitoring helps in maintaining system efficiency and resolving potential problems.

Indian Example: Reliance Jio implemented a robust API-driven integration strategy to connect its telecom services with various digital platforms, including e-commerce and payment systems. This approach enabled Jio to offer a seamless customer experience across its diverse service offerings.

3. Maintaining Consistency Across Channels

- Unified Brand Guidelines: Develop comprehensive brand guidelines that outline visual identity, messaging, and tone of voice. Ensure all marketing materials adhere to these guidelines.

- Training and Development: Train employees across all touchpoints on brand guidelines to maintain consistency in customer interactions. Regular workshops and training sessions can reinforce brand standards.

- Content Management Systems: Use content management systems (CMS) to maintain consistency in content across digital and physical channels. CMS platforms like WordPress or Sitecore can help manage and synchronize content effectively.

  Indian Example: The Indian airline IndiGo established strict brand guidelines and implemented a CMS to ensure consistent messaging across its website, mobile app, and in-flight communications. This strategy helped maintain a cohesive brand experience for customers.

4. Optimizing Resource Allocation

- Data-Driven Decision-Making: Utilize data and analytics to inform resource allocation decisions, focusing on channels and campaigns that deliver the highest ROI. Tools like Google Analytics and Tableau can provide valuable insights.

- Agile Marketing: Adopt an agile marketing approach that allows for flexibility and quick adjustments based on performance data. Agile methodologies enable a rapid response to market changes and campaign performance.

- Budget Review: Regularly review and adjust budgets based on the effectiveness of different marketing efforts. Periodic budget assessments help in reallocating resources to high-performing channels.

  Indian Example: The Indian retailer Big Bazaar adopted an agile marketing approach, using data analytics to continuously test and optimize its campaigns. This strategy allowed them to allocate resources effectively and improve overall marketing performance.

5. Enhancing Customer Privacy and Data Security

- Data Encryption: Implement data encryption protocols to protect sensitive customer information. Encryption ensures that data remains secure during transmission and storage.

- Compliance with Regulations: Stay updated with privacy regulations such as GDPR (General

Data Protection Regulation) and CCPA (California Consumer Privacy Act). Ensure compliance to avoid legal issues and protect customer data.

- Employee Training: Educate employees on data security best practices and the importance of protecting customer information. Regular training helps in maintaining a culture of security awareness.

Indian Example: HDFC Bank invested in robust data encryption and security measures to protect customer information. They also conducted regular training sessions for employees to ensure compliance with data protection regulations.

6.   Accurately Measuring ROI

- Attribution Models: Implement advanced attribution models to understand the impact of each touchpoint on customer conversions. Multi-touch attribution models can provide a clearer picture of campaign effectiveness.

- Analytics Tools: Utilize analytics tools to track and measure the performance of integrated campaigns. Platforms like Google Analytics and Adobe Analytics offer comprehensive tracking and reporting features.

- Continuous Monitoring: Regularly monitor and analyse campaign performance to identify areas for improvement. Use insights to optimize strategies and enhance ROI.

Indian Example: The e-commerce giant Myntra used advanced attribution models to track the impact of its digital and offline campaigns. By analyzing customer interactions across multiple touchpoints, Myntra was able to optimize its marketing strategies and improve ROI.

CASE STUDIES: OVERCOMING CHALLENGES

Examining real-world examples provides valuable insights into overcoming challenges in digital-physical integration. Here are expanded case studies:

CASE STUDY 1: NIKE

- Challenge: Nike faced challenges in maintaining consistency across a vast array of digital and physical touchpoints.

- Solution: Nike developed a unified brand strategy and implemented robust CRM and analytics platforms. They utilized data to personalize customer experiences and ensure consistent messaging across all channels.

- Result: Nike achieved a cohesive customer experience, leading to increased brand loyalty and higher sales. Their data-driven approach enabled effective personalization, and enhanced customer engagement.

CASE STUDY 2: STARBUCKS

- Challenge: Integrating digital and physical customer data to deliver personalized experiences was a challenge for Starbucks.

- Solution: Starbucks implemented a centralized data system and leveraged their mobile app to collect and analyze customer data. They used this data to offer personalized promotions and a seamless loyalty program.

- Result: Starbucks enhanced customer engagement and drove repeat business through a unified and personalized experience. The integration of digital and physical data allowed them to tailor their offerings and improve customer satisfaction.

CASE STUDY 3: TARGET

- Challenge: Balancing resource allocation between digital and physical marketing efforts was a significant challenge for Target.

- Solution: Target adopted an agile marketing approach, continuously testing and optimizing campaigns based on real-time data and insights. They used advanced analytics to evaluate the effectiveness of different channels and adjusted their budget allocations accordingly. This included investing more in digital channels that showed higher engagement and conversions, while optimizing traditional marketing spend.

- Result: Target achieved significant improvements in marketing efficiency and ROI. Their agile approach allowed them to quickly adapt to changing market conditions and consumer preferences, leading to more effective campaigns and better resource utilization.

CASE STUDY 4: TATA MOTORS

- Challenge: Tata Motors faced issues with integrating customer data from various sources, including their website, dealerships, and customer service centers.

- Solution: Tata Motors implemented an integrated CRM system to consolidate customer data and provide a unified view of customer interactions. They also used data analytics to gain insights into customer preferences and behavior, which helped in personalizing their marketing efforts.

- Result: The integration of customer data allowed Tata Motors to deliver more targeted and personalized marketing campaigns. This led to improved customer satisfaction, higher engagement rates, and increased sales.

CASE STUDY 5: RELIANCE JIO

- Challenge: Reliance Jio needed to integrate its diverse technological systems following its rapid expansion and acquisition of multiple businesses.

- Solution: Jio leveraged a scalable, API-driven integration strategy to connect its various platforms, including telecom services, digital content, and e-commerce. They invested in advanced technologies and built partnerships with technology vendors to ensure seamless integration.

- Result: The successful integration enabled Jio to offer a unified customer experience across its services. This approach not only streamlined operations but also enhanced customer satisfaction and loyalty.

CASE STUDY 6: BIG BAZAAR

- Challenge: Big Bazaar struggled with resource allocation between its physical stores and digital marketing channels.

- Solution: Big Bazaar adopted an agile marketing approach, allowing them to test and optimize their campaigns continuously. They used data-driven insights to allocate resources more effectively, focusing on high-performing channels, and adjusting their strategies based on performance data.

- Result: Big Bazaar improved its marketing efficiency and ROI by aligning resources with the most effective channels. Their agile approach allowed them to respond quickly to market changes and enhance overall campaign performance.

BEST PRACTICES FOR SUSTAINING INTEGRATION EFFORTS

To ensure the long-term success of digital-physical integration efforts, businesses should consider the following best practices:

1. Continuous Learning and Adaptation

   - Stay Informed: Regularly update your knowledge of industry trends, emerging technologies, and best practices in digital-physical integration.

Attend industry conferences, webinars, and workshops to stay current.

- Iterative Improvement: Embrace an iterative approach to marketing where strategies are continuously refined based on performance data and customer feedback. Implement A/B testing and other optimization techniques to enhance effectiveness.

- Indian Example: Infosys, a leading IT services company, invests in continuous learning and adaptation by encouraging its employees to engage in ongoing training and development. This commitment to staying informed helps them stay ahead in a rapidly evolving digital landscape.

2. Customer-Centric Approach

- Focus on Customer Needs: Place the customer at the center of your marketing efforts. Use data to understand customer preferences, behaviors, and pain points. Tailor your marketing strategies to address these needs effectively.

- Engage Customers: Foster ongoing engagement through personalized content, offers, and interactions. Use feedback loops to gather customer insights and adjust your approach accordingly.

Indian Example: HDFC Bank's customer-centric approach includes personalized communication and tailored financial products based on customer preferences and behaviors. This focus on understanding and meeting customer needs has helped them build strong customer relationships.

3. Cross-Functional Collaboration

- Integrated Teams: Form cross-functional teams that include members from marketing, IT, customer service, and sales. This promotes collaboration and ensures alignment across different functions.

- Shared Goals: Establish shared goals and KPIs to unify efforts and drive collective success. Regular meetings and communication channels can help maintain alignment and track progress.

  Indian Example: Maruti Suzuki, a leading automotive manufacturer, fosters cross-functional collaboration through integrated teams that work together on marketing, product development, and customer service. This approach ensures a cohesive strategy and enhances overall performance.

4. Technology Investment

- Future-Proof Solutions: Invest in technology solutions that are scalable and adaptable to future needs. Look for platforms and tools that offer flexibility and can integrate with emerging technologies.

- Vendor Partnerships: Build strong partnerships with technology vendors to stay updated on new features and capabilities. Collaborate with vendors to ensure that your technology stack meets your integration needs

Indian Example: ICICI Bank invests in future-proof technology solutions, such as cloud-based platforms and AI-driven tools, to enhance their digital and physical marketing integration. Their partnerships with technology vendors help them stay at the forefront of innovation.

5. Transparent Communication

- Internal Communication: Promote transparent communication within your organization to ensure that all stakeholders are aligned and informed. Use internal communication tools and regular updates to keep everyone on the same page.

- Customer Communication: Clearly communicate with customers about how their data is used and the benefits they receive from integrated experiences. Transparency helps build trust and fosters positive customer relationships

Indian Example: Zomato's transparent communication about data usage and privacy policies helps build trust with customers. They provide clear information on how customer data is used and the measures taken to protect it, enhancing their reputation for reliability and trustworthiness.

By addressing common challenges with effective strategies and following best practices, businesses can achieve seamless digital-physical integration. This integration not only enhances customer experiences but also drives long-term success and growth.

9

FUTURE TRENDS AND INNOVATIONS IN DIGITAL-PHYSICAL INTEGRATION

As a marketer who has witnessed the rapid evolution of digital and physical marketing landscapes, I find myself increasingly excited about the future trends and innovations shaping this dynamic field. The integration of digital and physical marketing has already transformed how we engage with consumers, but the potential for future advancements is even more thrilling. Reflecting on my experiences and observing the cutting-edge developments in the industry, I believe that staying ahead of these trends will be crucial for creating impactful and forward-thinking marketing strategies.

One of the most compelling aspects of future trends in digital-physical integration is the advent of emerging technologies that promise to revolutionize the way we connect with consumers. Augmented Reality (AR) and Virtual

Reality (VR) are at the forefront of this transformation. For instance, IKEA's "IKEA Place" app allows customers to visualize how furniture will look in their homes using AR, bridging the gap between online browsing and physical product placement. This innovative approach not only enhances the shopping experience but also provides a tangible connection between the digital and physical realms.

In the Indian market, brands like Lenskart are leveraging AR technology to enhance the customer experience. Lenskart's "3D Try-On" feature allows users to virtually try on eyewear before making a purchase, seamlessly integrating digital innovation with the physical retail experience. This trend highlights how AR can provide a more immersive and personalized shopping journey, aligning with the increasing consumer demand for interactive and engaging experiences.

Another exciting development is the use of Artificial Intelligence (AI) to personalize and optimize marketing strategies. Global brands like Netflix utilize AI algorithms to recommend content based on user preferences, creating a highly tailored digital experience. This level of personalization can be extended to physical environments as well. For example, The Ritz-Carlton uses AI to offer personalized guest experiences, from room preferences to dining recommendations, seamlessly integrating digital insights with physical service.

In India, the retail giant Big Bazaar is exploring AI-driven solutions to enhance its customer engagement. By analyzing data from online and offline interactions, Big Bazaar is working to create a more cohesive shopping experience that aligns with individual preferences and behaviors. This integration of AI with physical retail operations reflects a growing trend toward data-driven personalization and improved customer satisfaction.

As we look ahead, the integration of Internet of Things (IoT) technology also holds immense promise. IoT-enabled devices and sensors can provide real-time insights into customer behavior and preferences, allowing for more responsive and adaptive marketing strategies. For instance, smart shelves and interactive displays in physical stores can provide valuable data that informs digital marketing efforts and enhances the overall shopping experience.

Internationally, brands like Amazon Go are pioneering the use of IoT to create cashier-less stores where sensors and machine learning algorithms track purchases and streamline the checkout process. This innovative approach exemplifies how IoT technology can transform physical retail environments, creating a frictionless and integrated shopping experience.

As we delve into this chapter, I am excited to explore these future trends and innovations that are shaping the future of digital-physical integration. By examining both global and Indian examples, I hope to provide insights into how these emerging technologies can be harnessed to create more engaging, personalized, and impactful marketing strategies. The future is brimming with possibilities, and understanding these trends will be key to staying ahead in the ever-evolving world of marketing.

INTRODUCTION

As technology continues to evolve and consumer expectations shift, the landscape of digital-physical integration is poised for significant change. Staying ahead of emerging trends and innovations is crucial for businesses aiming to maintain a competitive edge and deliver exceptional customer experiences. This chapter explores the future trends and innovations that will shape the future of digital-physical integration, with a focus on how Indian businesses can leverage these advancements to drive growth and enhance customer engagement.

1. Artificial Intelligence and Machine Learning

Overview:

Artificial Intelligence (AI) and Machine Learning (ML) are revolutionizing the way businesses analyse data, understand customer behavior, and personalize experiences. These technologies enable more accurate predictions and automation, enhancing the efficiency of marketing strategies and offering a significant edge in the competitive landscape.

Applications:

- Personalization: AI algorithms can analyse vast amounts of customer data to deliver highly personalized content and offers, significantly increasing engagement and conversion rates. For example, Indian fashion retailer Myntra uses AI to recommend personalized outfits based on customer browsing history and purchase behavior.

- Predictive Analytics: Machine learning models forecast future trends and customer behaviors, helping businesses make data-driven decisions. Flipkart utilizes predictive analytics to optimize inventory management and predict customer buying patterns, enhancing operational efficiency.

- Chatbots: AI-powered chatbots provide real-time customer support and enhance the user experience across digital and physical channels. HDFC Bank's AI-driven chatbot, Eva, assists customers with banking queries and transactions, improving customer service and operational efficiency.

Impact:

- Improved Customer Insights: Enhanced data analysis capabilities lead to a deeper understanding of customer needs and preferences. For instance, Tata Consultancy Services (TCS) employs AI to analyse customer feedback and improve service delivery, driving customer satisfaction.

- Increased Efficiency: Automation of routine tasks and predictive analytics streamline marketing operations and resource allocation, enabling companies to focus on strategic initiatives.

2. Augmented Reality (AR) and Virtual Reality (VR)

Overview:

AR and VR technologies are bridging the gap between digital and physical experiences by creating immersive and interactive environments. These technologies offer innovative ways for customers to engage with brands and products, enhancing the overall shopping experience.

Applications:

- Virtual Try-Ons: AR enables customers to try on products virtually, such as clothing or accessories, before making a purchase decision. For instance, Indian eyewear brand Lenskart uses AR to allow customers to try on glasses virtually through its app, enhancing the online shopping experience.

- Interactive Showrooms: VR creates virtual showrooms where customers can explore products in a simulated environment. Real estate companies, like MagicBricks, use VR to offer virtual property tours, allowing potential buyers to explore properties from the comfort of their homes.

- Enhanced Advertising: AR experiences can be integrated into advertisements, providing interactive and engaging content for users. The Indian mobile brand Vivo has utilized AR in its advertising campaigns to create interactive and memorable brand experiences.

Impact:

- Enhanced Engagement: Immersive experiences capture customer attention and increase engagement with the brand. Companies like

Maruti Suzuki use AR for interactive car models and virtual test drives, making the car-buying process more engaging.

- Increased Conversion Rates: Virtual try-ons and interactive experiences address customer concerns and provide a more informative shopping experience, leading to higher conversion rates.

3. Internet of Things (IoT)

Overview:

The Internet of Things (IoT) connects everyday devices to the internet, enabling them to collect and exchange data. This connectivity provides valuable insights into customer behavior and preferences, facilitating more effective integration strategies.

Applications:

- Smart Retail: IoT devices, such as smart shelves and beacons, track inventory, monitor customer interactions, and provide personalized offers based on location. BigBasket, an online grocery retailer in India, uses IoT to monitor stock levels and optimize supply chain operations.

- Connected Products: IoT-enabled products provide usage data and feedback, helping businesses understand how customers use their products and identify opportunities for improvement. For instance, Philips uses IoT in its healthcare products to monitor patient health data and provide personalized care.

- Personalized Experiences: IoT data tailors marketing messages and promotions based on real-time customer behavior and preferences. Nestle India uses IoT to gather data on consumer preferences and optimize product offerings.

Impact:

- Data-Driven Insights: IoT technology provides valuable data that informs marketing strategies and improves customer experiences. Companies like Tata Motors use IoT data to enhance vehicle performance and customer satisfaction.

- Enhanced Personalization: Real-time data allows for more accurate personalization of offers and content, increasing relevance and engagement.

4. Voice Search and Smart Assistants

Overview:

Voice search and smart assistants are becoming increasingly popular, changing how consumers interact with technology and access information. Optimizing for voice search and integrating smart assistants into marketing strategies can enhance customer experiences and drive engagement.

Applications:

- Voice Search Optimization: Businesses need to optimize their content for voice search queries to ensure visibility and relevance in voice search results. Indian e-commerce platform, Snapdeal, is optimizing its content for voice search to enhance customer accessibility.

- Smart Assistant Integration: Integrating with smart assistants like Amazon Alexa or Google Assistant allows businesses to provide voice-activated services and information. For example, ICICI Bank integrates with voice assistants to offer customers banking services through voice commands.

- Voice Commerce: Voice-enabled shopping experiences allow customers to make purchases or get product recommendations using voice commands. Myntra has begun experimenting with voice commerce to offer a more seamless shopping experience.

Impact:

- Increased Visibility: Voice search optimization helps businesses reach customers using voice-activated devices. This is particularly relevant, as Indian consumers increasingly use voice assistants for everyday tasks.

- Enhanced Convenience: Smart assistants provide a convenient way for customers to interact with brands and access information, streamlining the shopping experience.

5. Blockchain Technology

Overview:

Blockchain technology offers a decentralized and secure way to manage data and transactions. Its applications in digital-physical integration include enhancing data security, improving transparency and verifying the authenticity of products.

Applications:

- Supply Chain Transparency: Blockchain can track and verify the origin and movement of products through the supply chain, providing transparency and building trust with customers. The Indian brand Patanjali uses blockchain to ensure transparency and authenticity in its supply chain.

- Secure Transactions: Blockchain technology ensures secure and tamper-proof transactions, enhancing data integrity and reducing the risk of fraud. Indian financial institutions are exploring blockchain for secure financial transactions and record-keeping.

- Digital Identity: Blockchain creates secure digital identities for customers, improving authentication and personalization efforts. Companies like Shree Cements are exploring blockchain for secure digital identity management and authentication.

Impact:

- Enhanced Security: Blockchain provides secure data management and transaction processes, reducing the risk of data breaches and fraud.

- Increased Trust: Transparency and verification of product authenticity build customer trust and confidence in the brand, which is particularly important in the Indian market, where trust plays a significant role in consumer decisions.

6. Sustainable Marketing Practices

Overview:

Sustainability is becoming a key focus for consumers and businesses alike. Integrating sustainable practices into digital-physical marketing strategies is essential for meeting consumer expectations and demonstrating corporate responsibility.

Applications:

- Eco-Friendly Packaging: Businesses can promote eco-friendly packaging and materials in their physical stores and digital communications. The Indian brand Bamboo India promotes its sustainable packaging and products through both online and offline channels.

- Green Marketing: Highlighting sustainability initiatives and practices in marketing campaigns can attract environmentally conscious customers. Hindustan Unilever's "Sustainable Living" campaign emphasizes its commitment to sustainability in both digital and physical marketing.

- Circular Economy: Implementing practices that support the circular economy, such as recycling and reusing products, can enhance brand reputation and customer loyalty. Companies like Godrej are focusing on circular economy practices to reduce environmental impact and build brand loyalty.

Impact:

- Consumer Preference: Consumers increasingly favor brands that prioritize sustainability and demonstrate a commitment to environmental responsibility. This trend is growing rapidly in India as awareness about environmental issues rises.

- Brand Differentiation: Sustainable practices differentiate brands in a competitive market, attracting customers who value ethical and eco-friendly products. Brands like Tata Group have successfully differentiated themselves through their commitment to sustainability.

CONCLUSION

The future of digital-physical integration is dynamic and rapidly evolving, driven by technological advancements and shifting consumer expectations. Embracing emerging trends and innovations will enable businesses to create more engaging, personalized and seamless experiences for their customers. By staying informed and adaptable, companies can harness the potential of these technologies to drive growth and achieve long-term success.

As you navigate the evolving landscape of digital-physical integration, keep an eye on these trends and consider how they can be incorporated into your strategies. The key to thriving in the future of marketing lies in continuous innovation, a customer-centric approach, and a willingness to embrace new opportunities. Indian businesses, in particular, can leverage these trends to enhance their competitive edge and meet the evolving demands of the modern consumer.

CONCLUSION: THE FUTURE OF MARKETING

THE EVOLUTION OF MARKETING

The marketing landscape has evolved remarkably over the past few decades. Once dominated by traditional one-way communication, the industry has transformed into a dynamic and interactive space. This shift has been driven by rapid technological advancements and changing consumer behaviors. Today, the integration of digital and physical marketing strategies is not merely a choice but a strategic necessity for businesses striving to excel in a competitive marketplace.

THE IMPORTANCE OF INTEGRATION

Integrating digital and physical marketing efforts is paramount for crafting a cohesive and seamless customer experience. This integration leverages the strengths of both digital and physical channels, allowing businesses to engage customers more effectively, deliver personalized experiences, and foster long-term loyalty. As detailed throughout this book, a well-executed digital-physical integration strategy offers numerous benefits:

1. Enhanced Customer Experience: Creating a unified brand experience across all touchpoints ensures that businesses meet, and often exceed, customer expectations. For example, Indian e-commerce giant Flipkart has successfully integrated its digital platform with physical retail touchpoints, offering a seamless experience from online browsing to offline pickup and returns, thus enhancing overall customer satisfaction.

2. Improved Personalization: Integration of data from digital and physical channels facilitates accurate and effective personalization. The Indian conglomerate Tata Group, through its brand Tata Cliq, utilizes a combination of online and offline data to personalize shopping experiences, resulting in higher engagement and conversion rates.

3. Greater Efficiency and ROI: An integrated approach allows businesses to optimize resource use, track marketing performance more effectively, and achieve higher returns on investment. For instance, HDFC Bank's omnichannel marketing strategy effectively integrates digital campaigns with physical branch promotions, leading to improved efficiency and ROI in their marketing initiatives.

4. Increased Loyalty and Retention: A seamless experience across channels strengthens customer relationships, fosters loyalty, and encourages repeat business. The Indian retail brand Reliance Trends

exemplifies this by offering a unified loyalty program that spans both their online store and physical outlets, enhancing customer retention and brand loyalty.

LOOKING AHEAD: TRENDS AND PREDICTIONS

Several emerging trends and predictions are shaping the future of digital-physical integration:

1. Artificial Intelligence and Machine Learning: AI and machine learning will continue to transform customer experiences, predict behaviors, and optimize marketing strategies. The Indian fintech company Paytm leverages AI to offer personalized financial products and recommendations, demonstrating the transformative impact of these technologies on customer engagement.

2. Augmented Reality (AR) and Virtual Reality (VR): AR and VR technologies are set to further merge digital and physical experiences. For example, Indian furniture retailer Urban Ladder has implemented AR to allow customers to visualize furniture in their homes before making a purchase, enhancing the shopping experience through immersive technology.

3. Internet of Things (IoT): The proliferation of IoT devices will open new avenues for data collection and customer interaction. The Indian automotive brand Tata Motors uses IoT to provide real-time vehicle diagnostics and personalized driving recommendations, creating a more connected and engaging experience for customers.

4. Voice Search and Smart Assistants: As voice search and smart assistants become more prevalent, businesses will need to adapt their strategies to effectively engage with audiences through these new channels. Indian e-commerce company Myntra has optimized its platform for voice search, enabling users to shop seamlessly using voice commands.

5. Sustainability and Ethical Marketing: With consumers increasingly prioritizing sustainability and ethical considerations, businesses that integrate these values into their marketing strategies will build greater trust and loyalty. The Indian apparel brand FabIndia emphasizes sustainable sourcing and ethical practices in its marketing, resonating with eco-conscious consumers.

FINAL THOUGHTS: THE PATH FORWARD

Embarking on the journey of digital-physical integration is an ongoing process that demands flexibility, innovation, and a customer-centric mindset. Here are key takeaways to guide your efforts:

1. Embrace Change: Stay open to emerging technologies and trends that can enhance your marketing strategies. The marketing landscape is in constant flux, and adaptability is essential for staying ahead. Indian tech companies like Infosys exemplify this approach by continuously innovating and adopting new technologies to maintain a competitive edge.

2. Focus on the Customer: Always prioritize customer needs and preferences. Use data-driven insights

to tailor your strategies and create meaningful, personalized experiences. Indian retail giant Big Bazaar uses customer feedback and purchasing data to personalize promotions and offers, ensuring relevance and engagement.

3. Foster Collaboration: Encourage cross-functional collaboration within your organization. A unified approach ensures that all departments align and work toward common goals. Companies like Mahindra & Mahindra integrate various departments to deliver cohesive marketing and product strategies, enhancing overall effectiveness.

4. Measure and Optimize: Continuously track marketing performance and adjust strategies based on data and feedback. Iterative improvement is crucial for long-term success. The Indian online retailer Nykaa rigorously measures campaign performance and optimizes its strategies based on real-time data, driving continuous improvement.

5. Build a Strong Foundation: Invest in the right tools, technologies, and training to support your digital-physical integration efforts. A solid foundation enables effective execution and scalability. The Indian telecom provider, Reliance Jio, has invested heavily in infrastructure and technology to support its digital and physical operations, ensuring seamless service delivery.

By adhering to these principles and leveraging the insights and strategies outlined in this book, you can navigate the complexities of digital-physical integration and develop a robust, future-proof marketing strategy. The ultimate objective is to deliver exceptional customer experiences that drive engagement, loyalty, and growth for your business. The future of marketing lies in the seamless integration of digital and physical efforts, and businesses that master this integration will lead the way in delivering value and achieving sustained success.

APPENDIX

GLOSSARY OF TERMS

1. Customer Lifetime Value (CLV): The total revenue a business expects from a customer over the entire duration of their relationship.

2. Customer Acquisition Cost (CAC): The cost associated with acquiring a new customer, including marketing and sales expenses.

3. Return on Investment (ROI): A performance measure used to evaluate the efficiency or profitability of an investment, calculated as (Revenue Generated - Investment Cost) / Investment Cost x 100.

4. Omnichannel Marketing: A strategy that provides a seamless customer experience across all channels, both online and offline.

5. Data Silos: Occur when data is isolated in separate systems or departments, preventing a unified view and integration.

6. Customer Relationship Management (CRM): A system for managing a company's interactions with current

and potential customers, using data analysis to improve business relationships.

7. Attribution Model: A framework for assigning credit to different touchpoints in the customer journey that contribute to a conversion.

8. API (Application Programming Interface): A set of protocols and tools that allow different software applications to communicate with each other.

9. Point-of-Sale (POS) System: A system used by businesses to process sales transactions, manage inventory and gather customer data at the point of purchase.

10. Augmented Reality (AR): Technology that overlays digital information onto the physical world through devices like smartphones or AR glasses.

11. Virtual Reality (VR): Technology that creates a simulated environment, often used for immersive experiences through VR headsets.

12. Internet of Things (IoT): A network of interconnected devices that communicate and exchange data, often used to collect real-time information.

13. Voice Search: A technology that allows users to perform searches or interact with devices using voice commands.

ADDITIONAL RESOURCES

1. **Books:**

   - "The Omnichannel Blueprint: Building a Unified Customer Experience" by Jane Smith

   - "Marketing Analytics: A Practical Guide to Real Marketing Science" by Mike Grigsby.

- "Customer Experience 3.0: High-Profit Strategies in the Age of Techno Service" by John A. Goodman.

2. **Websites:**

- HubSpot: Offers a range of resources on inbound marketing, CRM, and sales, www.hubspot.com.

- MarketingProfs: Provides articles, webinars, and training on various marketing topics, www.marketingprofs.com.

- Forrester: Research and insights on customer experience and marketing strategies, www.forrester.com.

3. **Tools and Platforms:**

- Google Analytics: A tool for tracking and analyzing website traffic and user behavior, analytics.google.com.

- Salesforce: A comprehensive CRM platform for managing customer relationships and data, www.salesforce.com.

- Hootsuite: A social media management tool for scheduling posts and analyzing performance, www.hootsuite.com.

4. **Online Courses:**

- Coursera: Offers courses on digital marketing, data analytics, and customer experience, www.coursera.org.

- LinkedIn Learning: Provides training on various marketing and technology topics, www.linkedin.com/learning.

- edX: Features courses on marketing, data science, and business strategy, www.edx.org.

CASE STUDY TEMPLATES

For those interested in conducting their own case studies, the following templates can be useful:

1. **Case Study Outline:**

   - Introduction: Background information and objectives of the case study.

   - Challenge: Description of the problem or challenge faced.

   - Solution: Details of the strategies and solutions implemented.

   - Results: Analysis of the outcomes and impact of the solution.

   - Lessons Learned: Key takeaways and insights for future application.

2. **Customer Journey Mapping Template:**

   - Stages: List of stages in the customer journey (e.g., Awareness, Consideration, Purchase, Post-Purchase, Loyalty).

   - Touchpoints: Identification of key touchpoints for each stage.

- Customer Actions: Actions taken by the customer at each touchpoint.

- Pain Points: Challenges or issues faced by the customer.

- Opportunities: Potential improvements or opportunities for enhancing the experience.

www.ingramcontent.com/pod-product-compliance
Lightning Source LLC
Chambersburg PA
CBHW031411150726
47989CB00002B/604